My Book of Marian Prayers

The Mother of God received the Holy Spirit together with the Apostles at Pentecost, the birth of the Church.

My Book of Marian Prayers

A Treasury in Honor of the Blessed Virgin Mary

Anthony M. Buono and
Rev. Francis Evans, *Editors*

Illustrated

CATHOLIC BOOK PUBLISHING CORP.
New Jersey

NIHIL OBSTAT: Rev. Stephen Prisk, S.T.L.
Censor Librorum

IMPRIMATUR: ✠ Kevin J. Sweeney, D.D.
Bishop of Paterson

September 7, 2023

(T-328)

Printed in China 23 HA 1
catholicbookpublishing.com

CONTENTS

INTRODUCTION

MARY'S "Yes" to the Angel Gabriel encapsulated the humility, trust, obedience, and faithfulness that Mary models for all of us. She was first the Mother of Jesus, Who from the Cross gave her to all of us as our Mother. What a precious gift she is to all of her children!

We have no greater intercessor with Jesus than the Blessed Mother. "To Jesus through Mary" are words to make our own and to act upon.

Saints through the ages have demonstrated their love and devotion to Our Lady and have shared words of wisdom for us to ponder.

St. Louis de Montfort said: "Mary is the safest, easiest, shortest, and most perfect way of approaching Jesus; we never give more honor to Jesus than when we honor His Mother."

Pope St. John Paul II offered: "From Mary, we learn to trust even when all hope seems gone. From Mary we learn to love Christ, her Son. Learn from her to be always faithful, to trust that God's Word to you will be fulfilled, and that nothing is impossible with God."

This treasury provides a variety of Marian prayers: for instance, some that show Our Lady the love and honor that are due her and others that seek her as a source of consolation. In some way, each will serve as a means to embrace her as a most welcome guide along the path to eternal life.

When the Blessed Virgin Mary completed the course of her life on earth, she was assumed into the glory of heaven.

POPULAR PRAYERS

The Hail Mary

HAIL Mary, full of grace, the Lord is with you; blessed are you among women, and blessed is the fruit of your womb, Jesus. Holy Mary, Mother of God, pray for us sinners now and at the hour of our death. Amen.

The Hail! Holy Queen

HAIL! Holy Queen, Mother of Mercy, our life, our sweetness, and our hope. To you do we cry, poor banished children of Eve. To you do we send up our sighs, mourning and weeping in this valley of tears. Turn then, O most gracious advocate, your eyes of mercy toward us; and after this our exile, show unto us the blessed fruit of your womb, Jesus. O clement! O loving! O sweet Virgin Mary!

℣. Pray for us, O Holy Mother of God.

℟. That we may be made worthy of the promises of Christ.

The Memorare

REMEMBER, O most gracious Virgin Mary,
that never was it known
that anyone who fled to your protection,
implored your help, or sought your intercession
was left unaided.
Inspired by this confidence,
I fly unto you, O Virgin of virgins, my Mother;

to you do I come,
before you I stand, sinful and sorrowful.
O Mother of the Word Incarnate,
despise not my petitions,
but in your mercy hear and answer me. Amen.

Partial indulgence

The Angelus

℣. The Angel of the Lord declared unto Mary.

℟. **And she conceived of the Holy Spirit.**

Hail Mary, etc.

℣. Behold the handmaid of the Lord.

℟. **Be it done unto me according to Your word.**

Hail Mary, etc.

℣. And the Word was made flesh.

℟. **And dwelt among us.**

Hail Mary, etc.

℣. Pray for us, O holy Mother of God.

℟. **That we may be made worthy of the promises of Christ.**

Let us pray. **Pour forth, we beseech You, O Lord, Your grace into our hearts, that we to whom the Incarnation of Christ, Your Son, was made known by the message of an Angel, may by His Passion and Cross be brought to the glory of His Resurrection, through the same Christ our Lord. Amen.**

Regina Caeli

(Said during Easter Time instead of the Angelus)

QUEEN of Heaven, rejoice, alleluia. For He Whom you merited to bear, alleluia. Has risen as He said, alleluia. Pray for us to God, alleluia.

℣. Rejoice and be glad, O Virgin Mary, alleluia.
℟. Because the Lord is truly risen, alleluia.

Let us pray. O God, Who by the Resurrection of Your Son, our Lord Jesus Christ, granted joy to the whole world, grant, we beg You, that, through the intercession of the Virgin Mary, His Mother, we may attain the joys of eternal life. Through the same Christ our Lord. Amen.

The Magnificat / The Canticle of Mary

MY SOUL proclaims the greatness of the Lord,
my spirit rejoices in God my Savior
for he has looked with favor on his lowly servant.
From this day all generations will call me blessed:
the Almighty has done great things for me,
and holy is his Name.
He has mercy on those who fear him
in every generation.
He has shown the strength of his arm,
he has scattered the proud in their conceit.
He has cast down the mighty from their thrones,
and has lifted up the lowly.

He has filled the hungry with good things,
and the rich he has sent away empty.
He has come to the help of his servant Israel
for he has remembered his promise of mercy,
the promise he made to our fathers,
to Abraham and his children for ever.

A *partial indulgence* is granted the faithful who devoutly recite the canticle called the *Magnificat*.

We Fly to Your Patronage / Sub Tuum Praesidium

WE FLY to your patronage,
O holy Mother of God;
despise not our petitions in our necessities,
but deliver us always from all dangers,
O glorious and blessed Virgin Mary.

LITANIES

Litany of Loreto

(See page 75 of The Holy Rosary.)

Litany to Our Lady of Fatima

(For Private Devotion)

OUR Lady of Fatima, pray for our dear country.
Our Lady of Fatima, sanctify our clergy.
Our Lady of Fatima, make our Catholics more fervent.
Our Lady of Fatima, guide and inspire those who govern us.
Our Lady of Fatima, cure the sick who confide in you.
Our Lady of Fatima, console the sorrowful who trust in you.
Our Lady of Fatima, help those who invoke your aid.
Our Lady of Fatima, deliver us from all dangers.
Our Lady of Fatima, help us to resist temptation.
Our Lady of Fatima, obtain for us all that we lovingly ask of you.
Our Lady of Fatima, help those who are dear to us.
Our Lady of Fatima, bring back to the right road all our erring brothers and sisters.
Our Lady of Fatima, give us back our ancient fervor.
Our Lady of Fatima, obtain for us pardon of our many sins and offenses.

Our Lady of Fatima, bring all people to the feet of your Divine Child.
Our Lady of Fatima, obtain peace for the world.
O Mary conceived without sin, pray for us who have recourse to you.
Immaculate Heart of Mary, pray for us now and at the hour of our death. Amen.

Let us pray.

O God of infinite goodness and mercy,
fill our hearts with a great confidence in Your dear Mother,
whom we invoke under the title of
Our Lady of the Rosary and Our Lady of Fatima,
and grant us by her powerful intercession all the graces,
spiritual and temporal, which we need.
Through Christ our Lord.

℟. Amen.

Litany to Our Lady of Good Counsel

(For Private Devotion)

LORD, have mercy.
Christ, have mercy.
Lord, have mercy.
Christ, hear us.
Christ, graciously hear us.

God the Father of heaven, *have mercy on us.**
God the Son, Redeemer of the world,

* *Have mercy on us* is repeated after each invocation.

God the Holy Spirit,
Holy Trinity, one God,

Beloved Daughter of the Eternal Father, *pray for us.***
August Mother of God the Son,
Blessed Spouse of God the Holy Spirit,
Living temple of the Holy Trinity,
Queen of heaven and earth,
Seat of Divine Wisdom,
Depositary of the secrets of the Most High,
Virgin most prudent,
In our doubts and difficulties,
In our tribulations and anguish,
In our discouragements,
In perils and temptations,
In all our undertakings,
In all our needs,
At the hour of death,
By your Immaculate Conception,
By your happy nativity,
By your admirable Presentation,
By your glorious Annunciation,
By your charitable Visitation,
By your Divine Maternity,
By your holy Purification,
By the sorrows and anguish of thy maternal heart,
By your precious death,
By your triumphant Assumption,

** *Pray for us* is repeated after each invocation.

Lamb of God, You take away the sins of the world; *spare us, O Lord.*

Lamb of God, You take away the sins of the world; *graciously hear us, O Lord.*

Lamb of God, You take away the sins of the world; *have mercy on us.*

℣. Pray for us, O holy Mother of God.

℟. *And obtain for us the gift of good counsel.*

Let us pray.

Lord Jesus, Author and Dispenser of all good,
Who in becoming incarnate in the womb of the Blessed Virgin
has communicated to her lights above those
of all the Heavenly intelligences,
grant that in honoring her
under the title of Our Lady of Good Counsel,
we may merit always to receive from her goodness
counsels of wisdom and salvation,
which will conduct us to the port of a blessed eternity.
Amen.

Biblical Litany of Our Lady

It is possible to compose a long list of praises of the Virgin Mary by using God's own Word. They are concrete titles, attributed to her and emphasizing the Most Blessed Virgin's "function" in the mystery of the Word made flesh and the Mystical Body. When we call upon Mary by these titles, we are praying with the Word of God that has been from time to time interpreted by the Church's tradition in a clearly Marian sense. The litany that follows here was composed by A. M. Roguet and was published by La Vie Spirituelle, *n. 553, pp. 213-217.*

GREETED by the Angel Gabriel: Lk 1:28.
Full of Grace: *ibid.*
Mother of Jesus: Lk 1:31.
Mother of the Son of the Most High: Lk 1:32.
Mother of the son of David: *ibid.*
Mother of the King of Israel: Lk 1:33.
Mother by act of the Holy Spirit: Lk 1:35; Mt 1:20.
Handmaid of the Lord: Lk 1:38.
Virgin, Mother of Emmanuel: Mt 1:23, citing Is 7:14; cf. Mt 5:2.
You in whom the Word became flesh: Jn 1:14.
You in whom the Word dwelt among us: *ibid.*
Blessed among all women: Lk 1:41; cf. Jud 13:18.
Mother of the Lord: Lk 1:43.
Happy are you who have believed in the words uttered by the Lord: Lk 1:43.
Lowly handmaid of the Lord: Lk 1:48.
Called blessed by all generations: *ibid.*
You in whom the Almighty worked wonders: *ibid.*
Heiress of the promises made to Abraham: Lk 1:55.
Mother of the new Isaac: Lk 1:37 (Gen 18:14).
You who gave birth to your firstborn at Bethlehem: Lk 2:7.
You who wrapped your Child in swaddling clothes and laid Him in a manger: *ibid.*
Woman from whom Jesus was born: Gal 4:4; Mt 1:16, 21.

Mother of the Savior: Lk 2:11; Mt 1:21.
Mother of the Messiah: Lk 2:11; Mt 1:16.
You who were found by the shepherds with Joseph and the newborn Child: Lk 2:16.
You who kept and meditated on all things in your heart: Lk 2:19.
You who offered Jesus in the Temple: Lk 2:22.
You who put Jesus into the arms of Simeon: Lk 2:28.
You who marveled at what was said of Jesus: Lk 2:33.
You whose soul a sword should pierce: Lk 2:35.
Mother who were found together with the Child by the Wise Men: Mt 2:11.
Mother whom Joseph took into refuge in Egypt: Mt 2:14.
You who took the Child Jesus to Jerusalem for the Passover: Lk 2:42.
You who searched for Jesus for three days: Lk 2:46.
You who found Jesus again in His Father's house: Lk 2: 46-49.
Mother whom Jesus obeyed at Nazareth: Lk 2:51.
Model of widows: Cf. Mk 6:3.
Jesus' companion at the marriage feast at Cana: Jn 2:1-2.
You who told the servants, "Do as He shall tell you": Jn 2:5.
You who gave rise to Jesus' first miracle: Jn 2:11.
Mother of Jesus for having done the Will of the Father in heaven: Mt 12:50.

Blessed for having heard the word of God and kept it: Lk 11:28.
Mother standing at the foot of the Cross: Jn 19:25.
Mother of the disciple whom Jesus loved: Jn 19: 26-27.
Queen of the Apostles, persevering in prayer with them: Acts 1:14.
Woman clothed with the sun: Rev 12:1.
Woman crowned with twelve stars: *ibid.*
Sorrowful Mother of the Church: Rev 12:2.
Glorious Mother of the Messiah: Rev 12:5.
Image of the new Jerusalem: Rev 21:2.
River of living water, flowing from the throne of God and the Lamb: Rev 22:1; cf. Ps 45:5.

Our Lady of Perpetual Help inspires confidence in those who seek her intercession in times of need.

NOVENAS

Our Lady of Perpetual Help

Meditation

THE miraculous picture of Madonna and Child rests on the main altar of the church of the Redemptorist Fathers in Rome. It was first in the possession of a wealthy Cretan merchant, then brought to Rome and eventually enthroned in St. Matthew's Church. For three hundred years crowds of pilgrims have journeyed far to see this picture, the source of many cures. In 1812, St. Matthew's Church was razed, and for fifty-four years the picture's location was not known. When it was found, Pope Pius IX gave it to the Redemptorist Fathers for their church on the spot where Mary first had been revered in this special manner as Our Lady of Perpetual Help.

The miraculous picture is painted like an icon. Two Angels designated as Sts. Michael and Gabriel are seen beside the Virgin's head, carrying in their veiled hands the instruments of Christ's Passion, the Cross, the spear, and the sponge. The picture was probably painted by a Greek artist of the thirteenth or fourteenth century.

Mary is invoked as Our Lady of Perpetual Help because she affords help to Christians even in all temporal needs. Although she is now enthroned in heaven, she still takes an interest in our misery and relieves our wants.

Mary brings us help especially in our spiritual needs. She is a most merciful Mother who rejects no sinner. She lovingly interests herself in our behalf and tries to reconcile us to her Son when we have sinned. She assists us in temptation. She confirms us in good and obtains for us the grace of making progress in the path of virtue, for she desires nothing more ardently than that we all become partakers of the fruits of redemption, won for us by her Son. In our efforts to reach holiness, she supports us and obtains for us the grace of perseverance. We can ask nothing of her that will give her greater pleasure or that she will grant more willingly than the grace to do good.

Above all, Mary will assist us in the hour of death, which is a crucial moment in our life because it is then that we prepare for the judgment. As the exalted Queen of Heaven she takes the souls of her faithful servants under her protecting mantle, accompanies them to the judgment seat of her Son, and there she becomes their intercessor.

Mary is still the Mother of God in heaven as she was on earth; Jesus, Who is omnipotence itself, remains her Son for all eternity. Her love for us is now even more intense and more compassionate, because she knows our misery better in heaven. She obtains gentle rest for all who are laden with trouble and pain; she gives comfort to the afflicted and healing to the sick.

Mary is our Mother of Perpetual Help, and therefore we should have an unbounded confidence in her. She can help us, for her prayer is all-powerful with God, and she will help us, for she is our Mother and she loves us as her children.

The Word of God

"Can a woman forget the infant at her breast; or feel no compassion for the child of her womb? Even should she forget, I will never forget you." *—Isa 49:15*

"When the wine was exhausted, ... [Jesus'] mother said to the servants, 'Do whatever he tells you.' " *—Jn 2:3-5*

"Blessed is the one who listens to me, who keeps watch daily at my gates, ... For whoever finds me finds life and receives favor from the LORD." *—Prov 8:34-35*

Novena Prayers

Novena Prayer

MOTHER of Perpetual Help, behold at your feet a sinner who has recourse to you and has confidence in you. Mother of Mercy, have pity on me. I hear all calling you the refuge and hope of sinners. Be, then, my refuge and my hope. For the love of Jesus Christ, your Son, help me.

Give your hand to a poor sinner who commends himself to you and dedicates himself to your lasting service. I praise and thank God Who in His mercy has given to me this confidence in you, a sure pledge of my eternal salvation.

It is true that in the past, I, miserable and wretched, have fallen into sin because I did not have recourse to you. But I know that with your help I shall be able to overcome myself. I know, too, that you will help me, if I commend myself to you. But I fear that in the occasions of sin, I may neglect to call upon you and thus run the risk of being lost.

This grace, then, I seek of you; for this I implore you as much as I know how and as much as I can: that in all the attacks of hell I may ever have recourse to you and say to you: "O Mary, help me. O Mother of Perpetual Help, do not let me lose my God." *3 Hail Marys*

Mother of Perpetual Help, aid me ever to call upon your powerful name, since your name is the help of the living and the salvation of the dying. Mary most pure, Mary most sweet, grant that your name from this day forth may be to me the very breath of life. Dear Lady, do not delay in coming to help me when I call upon you, for in all the temptations that trouble me, in all the needs of my life, I will ever call upon you, repeating: "Mary, Mary."

What comfort, what sweetness, what confidence, what consolation fills my soul at the sound of your name, at the very thought of you! I give thanks to our Lord, Who for my sake has given you a name so sweet, so lovable and so mighty. But I am not content only to speak your name; I will call upon you because I love you. I want that love to remind me always to call you Mother of Perpetual Help. *3 Hail Marys*

Mother of Perpetual Help, you are the dispenser of every grace that God grants us in our misery. For this reason He has made you so powerful, so rich, and so kind that you might help us in our needs. You are the advocate of the most wretched and abandoned sinners, if they but come to you. Come to my aid, for I commend myself to you.

In your hands I place my eternal salvation; to you I entrust my soul. Count me among your most faithful servants. Take me under your protection; that is enough for me. If you protect me, I shall fear nothing. I shall not fear my sins, because you will obtain for me their pardon and remission. Neither shall I fear the evil spirits, because you are mightier than all the powers of hell.

I fear only that through my own negligence I may forget to recommend myself to you and so lose my soul. My dear Lady, obtain for me the forgiveness of my sins, love for Jesus, final perseverance, and the grace to have recourse to you at all times, Mother of Perpetual Help.

3 Hail Marys

(Saint Alphonsus Liguori)

Our Lady of Lourdes

Meditation

BETWEEN February 11 and July 16, 1858, the Blessed Virgin came down from heaven eighteen times and showed herself at Lourdes to Bernadette Soubirous a little girl of fourteen years of age. On February 11, while gathering wood, Bernadette heard a whistle of wind. With astonished eyes she saw a niche in the upper part of a rock filled with golden light, and there in the midst of it stood a Lady of great beauty.

Her robe glowed with the whiteness of snow in the sunshine and swept in majestic folds to the ground. Her head and shoulders were framed by a white veil, which fell the full length of her robe. A blue sash encircled her waist, and its two ends, wide and unornamented, reached down in front almost to her feet. Each of her feet bore a rose of purest gold. A rosary, whose beads were white and whose cross and chain were of gold, hung from her right arm. Her hands were open, and her arms outstretched slightly in front.

In her apparitions our Lady appealed for penance and prayers for sinners. On March 25, the feast of the Annunciation, the Blessed Mother declared her name to Bernadette and to the world. On that day Bernadette made this request: "My Lady, would you be so kind as to tell me who you are?"

This is how Bernadette describes what happened in that last apparition: "Three times I asked the Apparition her name. At the third instance, she stretched out her hands, which until then she held joined, raised them, and she said: 'I am the Immaculate Conception.'" Then having completed her great message to the world, the Lady smiled on Bernadette and withdrew without further word of farewell.

Less than four years before these apparitions, on December 8, 1854, Pope Pius IX proclaimed that Mary in the first instant of her conception was preserved free from all stain of original sin through the merits of her Divine Son. At Lourdes the Virgin Mary had come to confirm the infallible utterance of God's Vicar on earth and declared herself not only immaculately conceived, but "the Immaculate Conception."

On October 30, 1867, Bernadette made her religious profession in the Convent of the Congregation of the Sisters of Nevers, France. In January 1873, Bernadette became ill.

On April 16, about three in the afternoon, Bernadette prayed: "Holy Mary, Mother of God, pray for me, a poor sinner!" She made a Sign of the Cross, took the glass that was handed to her, twice swallowed a few drops of water, and then bending her head gently gave up her soul to her Creator.

Bernadette died, worn out with physical suffering, on April 16, 1879, at the age of thirty-six.

Now her incorrupt body can be seen as she lay in death in the side chapel of the motherhouse of the Sisters of Charity at Nevers, where she lived and died as Sister Marie Bernard. Thirty years after her death her body was found in a perfect state of preservation, undoubtedly a token of love of the Immaculate Virgin Mary. She was beatified in 1925, and on December 8, 1933, she was canonized by Pope Pius XI. Her feast day is February 18.

The Word of God

"You care for the earth and water it, making it most fertile." *—Ps 65:10*

"I have chosen and consecrated this house so that my name may be there forever and my eyes and my heart shall constantly be there." *—2 Chr 7:16*

"[I was] delighting in the children of men." *—Prov 8:31*

Novena Prayers

Novena Prayer

MARY, Mother of God, I firmly believe in the doctrine of Holy Mother Church concerning your Immaculate Conception: namely, that you were, in the first instant of your conception, by the singular grace and privilege of God, in view of the merits of Jesus Christ, the Savior of the human race, preserved immune from all stain of original sin.

Alone of all the children of Adam, you were gifted with the fullness of sanctifying grace that made you the object of a very special love on the part of God. How wonderful were the workings of Divine power to make you a fitting dwelling for the Redeemer of the world! With no tendency to evil, but with a deep yearning for the highest virtue, you glorified God more than all His other creatures. At the very instant of your conception your mind was filled with the light of God, and your will was entirely conformed to the Divine Will. You were always intimately united with God.

I thank God with you for these wonderful blessings. Help me to imitate your holiness to some degree. Your holiness was not the result of the privilege of your Immaculate Conception and sanctifying grace alone, but followed from your gift of yourself to God and your constant cooperation with His graces. Help me to be generous with God by turning to good account the graces that He ever bestows on me, and by rising promptly when I fall, with renewed confidence in His mercy.

Ever Immaculate Virgin, Mother of Mercy, health of the sick, refuge of sinners, comfort of the afflicted, you know my wants, my troubles, my sufferings. Deign to cast upon me a look of mercy.

By appearing in the Grotto of Lourdes, you were pleased to make it a privileged sanctuary, from which you dispense your favors; and already many sufferers have obtained the cure of their infirmities, both spiritual and corporal. I come, therefore, with the most unbounded confidence to implore your maternal intercession.

Obtain, O loving Mother, the granting of my requests. Through gratitude for your favors, I will endeavor to imitate your virtues that I may one day share your glory.

Through your loving compassion shown to thousands of pilgrims who come to your shrine at Lourdes, and through your special love for your devoted client Bernadette, I ask for this grace if it be the Will of God. *(Mention your request.)*

Our Lady of Lourdes, aid me through your prayer with your Divine Son, to be a true child of yours, as Bernadette was, and to grow daily into your likeness.

Prayer to Saint Bernadette

SAINT Bernadette, little shepherdess of Lourdes, favored with eighteen apparitions of the Immaculate Virgin Mary and with the privilege of lovingly conversing with her, now that you are eternally enjoying the entrancing beauty of the Immaculate Mother of God, do not forsake me, your devoted client, who am still in this valley of tears.

Intercede for me that I, too, may walk the simple paths of faith. Help me to imitate your example, at our heavenly Queen's request, by saying the Rosary daily and by doing penance for sinners.

Teach me to imitate your wonderful devotedness to God and our Lady, the Immaculate Conception, so that, like you, I may be blessed with the grace of lasting faithfulness and enjoy the happiness in heaven of the eternal vision of God the Father, Son, and Holy Spirit. Amen.

Prayer

GOD of infinite mercy, we celebrate the feast of Mary, Our Lady of Lourdes, the sinless Mother of God. May her prayers help us to rise above our human weakness. We ask this through our Lord Jesus Christ, Your Son, Who lives and reigns with You and the Holy Spirit, God, forever and ever. Amen.

The Immaculate Heart of the Blessed Virgin Mary

Meditation

ANY form of veneration of the Blessed Virgin is always directed to her person. So, too, in venerating the Immaculate Heart of Mary, we revere not only the real physical Heart of our Blessed Mother, but also her person as the source and bearer of all her virtues. We expressly honor her Heart as a symbol of her love for God and for people.

The first impulses to the veneration of the Immaculate Heart of Mary are found in Holy Scripture. After the arrival of the shepherds to the crib we read: "Mary treasured all these words and pondered them in her heart" (Lk 2:19).

After Mary and Joseph found the twelve-year-old Jesus in the Temple, Scripture says: "He went down with them and came to Nazareth, and he was obedient to them. His mother pondered all these things in her heart" (Lk 2:51).

At the Presentation of Jesus in the Temple, Simeon predicted: "And you yourself a sword will pierce" (Lk 2:35). These words were verified beneath the Cross, for as the Heart of Jesus was pierced by a lance, the Heart of His Blessed Mother was transfixed by the sword of sorrow. The Heart of Jesus had its first beat in the shelter of the most pure Heart of His Mother Mary, and this most pure Heart had also received in spirit the last beat of the Heart of Jesus. If the Sacred Heart would not be without the loving Heart of His Mother in heaven, He did not wish to be honored apart from her upon earth.

In one of the first apparitions at Fatima in 1917, our Lady said that Lucy must remain on earth a while longer to spread devotion to the Immaculate Heart of Mary.

In the third apparition at Fatima, July 13, 1917, our Lady told Lucy: "Our Lord wishes that devotion to my Immaculate Heart be established in the world. If what I tell you is done, many souls will be saved and there will be peace; the war will end. . . . I ask the consecration of Russia to my Immaculate Heart and Communion of reparation on the First Saturday of each month. . . . If my requests are granted, Russia will be converted and there will be peace. . . . In the end my Immaculate Heart will triumph, and an era of peace will be conceded to humanity."

On October 31, 1942, Pope Pius XII consecrated the world to the Immaculate Heart of Mary. The same Pope consecrated Russia to our Lady in 1952. The consecration of the world was renewed by Pope St. Paul VI in 1964 and by Pope St. John Paul II in 1981.

Shortly before Jacinta died at the age of ten, she said to Lucy, "I have only a short time left before I go to heaven, but you must remain here below to make the world know that our Lord wishes devotion to the Immaculate Heart of Mary established in the world. . . . Tell everybody that God gives graces through the Immaculate Heart of Mary. Tell them to ask these graces from her, and that the Heart of Jesus wishes to be venerated together with the Immaculate Heart of His Mother. Ask them to plead for peace from the Immaculate Heart of Mary, for the Lord has confided the peace of the world to her."

In obedience to her ecclesiastical superior and her confessor, Lucy revealed a part of the secret confided by our Lady, and it concerns the devotion to the Immaculate Heart of Mary.

Pope Pius XII instituted the feast of the Immaculate Heart of Mary in 1945, to be celebrated on August 22. Today this feast is celebrated on the Saturday after the Second Sunday after Pentecost.

The Word of God

"The king's daughter is adorned in robes threaded with gold." *—Ps 45:14*

"She is the reflection of eternal light, the spotless mirror of the active power of God and the image of his goodness." *—Wis 7:26*

"His mother pondered all these things in her heart." *—Lk 2:51*

Novena Prayers

Novena Prayer

IMMACULATE Heart of Mary, full of love for God and mankind, and of compassion for sinners, I consecrate myself entirely to you. I entrust to you the salvation of my soul. May my heart be ever united with yours, so that I may hate sin, love God, and my neighbor, and reach eternal life together with those whom I love.

Mediatrix of All Graces and Mother of Mercy, remember the infinite treasure that your Divine Son has merited by His sufferings and that He has confided to you for us, your children. Filled with confidence in your Motherly Heart, which I venerate and love, I come to you with my pressing needs. Through the merits of your loving Heart, and for the sake of the Sacred Heart of

Jesus, obtain for me the favor I ask. *(Mention your request.)*

Dearest Mother, if what I ask for should not be according to God's Will, pray that I may receive that which will be of greater benefit to my soul. May I experience the kindness of your Motherly Heart and the power of your intercession with Jesus during life and at the hour of my death. Amen.

Petitions

IMMACULATE Virgin, conceived without sin, you directed every movement of your most pure Heart toward God and were always obedient to His Divine Will. Obtain for me the grace to hate sin with all my heart and to learn from you to live in perfect resignation to the Will of God.

Mary, I admire that deep humility that troubled your blessed Heart at the message of the Angel Gabriel when he announced that you had been chosen to be the Mother of the Son of the Most High God. You considered yourself only God's lowly handmaid. Ashamed at the sight of my own pride, I beg of you the grace of a contrite and humble heart so that I may acknowledge my misery and reach the glory promised to the truly humble of heart.

Blessed Virgin, you kept in your Heart the precious treasure of the words of Jesus, your Son, and, pondering over the sublime mysteries they contained, you lived only for God. How ashamed I am of my coldness of heart! Dear Mother, obtain for me the grace of meditating always on the holy law of God and of seeking to follow your example in the fervent practice of all the Christian virtues.

Glorious Queen of Martyrs, during the Passion of your Son your holy Heart was cruelly pierced by the sword that had been foretold by the holy and aged Simeon. Obtain for my heart true courage and holy patience to bear the sufferings and trials of this difficult life. May I prove to be your true child by crucifying my flesh and all its desires in the mortification of the Cross.

Mary, Mystical Rose, your amiable Heart, burning with the living fire of love, adopted us as your children at the foot of the Cross, and you thereby became our most tender Mother. Let me feel the sweetness of your Motherly Heart and the power of your intercession with Jesus, in all the dangers that I meet with during life, and especially at the dread hour of my death. May my heart be ever united to yours and love Jesus now and forever. Amen.

Prayer

HEAVENLY Father, You prepared the Heart of the Virgin Mary to be a fitting dwelling place for Your Holy Spirit. By her prayers for us, may our souls become a more worthy temple of Your glory. Grant this through our Lord Jesus

Christ, Your Son, Who lives and reigns with You and the Holy Spirit, God, forever and ever. Amen.

The Assumption of the Blessed Virgin Mary

Meditation

THE Blessed Virgin Mary obeyed the law of *death*, but her death was rather a peaceful slumber, a gentle separation of the soul from the body. Her soul reached such a degree of love that it seemed unable to rest any longer, except in the blissful embrace of the Blessed Trinity. It left her immaculate body and sped to enjoy the blessed vision of God. But soon her beautiful soul was again united to her body which lay peacefully in the tomb, and suddenly Mary stood immortal and glorified, clothed in queenly glory.

As Angels sang their hymns of praise, Mary was *raised on high* to the Kingdom of glory by God's own power. Who can tell the joy of that loving embrace whereby Jesus welcomed and admitted His own Virgin Mother to unending union with Him in the glory of heaven!

Mary's peaceful tomb had been opened by the Apostles and found to be empty. Tradition tells us that beautiful flowers filled the place where her body had once lain, and heavenly music enveloped her empty tomb. The Apostles then realized that she had been taken up into heaven, soul and body.

It was *fitting* that Mary should be assumed into heaven with soul and body. By her Assumption God honored her body that was always the temple in which He dwelt by grace. It was a gate through which the Son of God, the Divine Word, passed to earth and became Man.

It was *fitting* that Mary's holy and virginal body that gave flesh and blood to the God of all sanctity, the Victor over death, should never experience the corruption of the grave. Death and corruption are a result of original sin; but by her Immaculate Conception, Mary was preserved from original sin and its effects.

Mary offered herself to suffering and her beloved Son to death for the redemption of mankind; it was *fitting* that she should be united with Him in glory.

We should rejoice that after years of suffering on earth, Mary has at last been taken to the throne prepared for her in heaven, where she reigns with her Son. The Church expresses this joy on the Solemnity of the Assumption of the Blessed Virgin Mary, August 15, which is also a Holyday of Obligation.

The Word of God

"We know that if the earthly tent in which we live is destroyed, we have a dwelling prepared for us by God, a dwelling in the heavens, not made with human hands, that will be eternal." *—2 Cor 5:1*

"A great sign appeared in heaven: a woman clothed with the sun, with the moon beneath her feet, and a crown of twelve stars on her head." *—Rev 12:1*

Novena Prayers

Novena Prayer

MARY, Queen assumed into heaven, I rejoice that after years of heroic martyrdom on earth, you have at last been taken to the throne prepared for you in heaven by the Holy Trinity.

Lift my heart with you in the glory of your Assumption above the dreadful touch of sin and impurity. Teach me how small earth becomes when viewed from heaven. Make me realize that death is the triumphant gate through which I shall pass to your Son, and that someday my body shall rejoin my soul in the unending bliss of heaven.

From this earth, over which I tread as a pilgrim, I look to you for help. In honor of your Assumption into heaven, I ask for this favor. *(Mention your request.)*

When my hour of death has come, lead me safely to the presence of Jesus to enjoy the vision of my God for all eternity together with you.

Prayer to Mary, Assumed into Heaven

MARY, my dear Mother and mighty Queen, take and receive my poor heart with all its freedom and desires, all its love and all the virtues and graces with which it may be adorned. All I am, all I might be, all I have and hold in the order of nature as well as of grace, I have received from God through your loving intercession, my Lady and Queen. Into your sovereign hands I entrust all, that it may be returned to its noble origin.

Mary, Queen of every heart, accept all that I am and bind me to you with the bonds of love, that I may be yours forever, and may be able to say in all truth: "I belong to Jesus through Mary."

My Mother, Assumed into Heaven, I love you. Give me a greater love for Jesus and for you.

Mary, Assumed into Heaven and Queen of the Universe, ever-Virgin Mother of God, obtain peace and salvation for us through your prayers, for you have given birth to Christ the Lord, the Savior of all mankind.

Prayer

ALMIGHTY, ever-living God, You raised to eternal glory the body and soul of the Immaculate Virgin Mary, Mother of Your Son. Grant that our minds may always be directed heavenward and that we may deserve to share in her glory.

Our Lady of Sorrows

Meditation

THE Seven Sorrows of the Blessed Virgin Mary that have made the strongest appeal to devotion are these: the prophecy of Simeon; the flight into Egypt; the three days' loss of Jesus; the meeting with Jesus carrying His Cross; His Death on Calvary; His being taken down from the Cross; and His burial in the tomb.

Simeon foretold to Jesus' Mother the opposition the Redeemer would arouse. When she offered her forty-day-old Child to God in the Temple, he said, "This child is destined for the fall and rise of many in Israel, and to be a sign that will be opposed, . . . and you yourself a sword will pierce" (Lk 2:34-35).

Mary's sorrow on Calvary was deeper than any sorrow ever felt on earth, for no mother in all the world had a heart as tender as the Heart of the Mother of God. As there was no love like her love, there was no sorrow like her sorrow. She bore her sufferings for us that we might enjoy the graces of Redemption. She suffered willingly in order to prove her love for us, for true love is proved by sacrifice.

It was not because she was the Mother of God that Mary could bear her sorrows, but because she saw things from His point of view and not from her own—or rather, she had made His point of view hers. We should do the same. The Mother of Sorrows will be on hand to help us.

Devotion to the Sorrows of Mary is the source of great graces because it leads into the depths of the Heart of Christ. If we think frequently of the false pleasures of this world, we shall embrace patiently the sorrows and sufferings of this life, and we shall be penetrated with a sorrow for sin.

The Church urges us to give ourselves over to the love of Mary completely and bear our cross patiently with the Mother of Sorrows. She earnestly wants to help us to bear our daily crosses because it was on Calvary that her dying Son entrusted us to her care. It was His last Will that she should be our Mother. It was also His last Will that we love His Mother as He did.

The Word of God

" 'This child is destined for the fall and rise of many in Israel, and to be a sign that will be opposed, so that the secret thoughts of many will be revealed, and you yourself a sword will pierce.' " *—Lk 2:34-35*

"His mother said to [Jesus]: 'Son, why have you done this to us? Your father and I have been searching for you with great anxiety.' " *—Lk 2:48*

"All of you who pass this way, look and see. Is there any sorrow like the sorrow that has been inflicted upon me . . .?" *—Lam 1:12*

Novena Prayers

Novena Prayer

MOST holy and afflicted Virgin, Mother of Sorrows and Queen of Martyrs! You stood motionless at the foot of the Cross beneath your dying Son. Through the sword of grief that pierced you then, through the unceasing suffering of your life of sorrow, and the bliss that now fully repays you for your past trials and afflictions, look upon me with a mother's tenderness and have pity on me, as I pray before you to venerate your sorrows, and place my request with childlike confidence in the sanctuary of your wounded Heart.

I beg of you to present to Jesus Christ, in union with the infinite merits of His Passion and Death, your sufferings at the foot of the Cross, and through the power of both, to grant my request. *(Mention your request.)*

To whom shall I turn in my needs and miseries, if not to you, Mother of Mercy? You drank so deeply of the chalice of your Son that you can sympathize with the sufferings of those who are still in this valley of tears.

Offer to our Divine Savior the sufferings He bore on the Cross that the memory of them may draw His mercy upon me, a sinner. Refuge of sinners and hope of all mankind, accept my petition and grant it, if it be according to the Will of God.

Lord Jesus Christ, I offer You the merits of Mary, Your Mother and ours, as she stood beneath the Cross, in order that by her loving intercession I may obtain the happy fruits of Your Passion and Death.

Offering

MARY, most holy Virgin and Queen of Martyrs, accept the sincere homage of my childlike love. Into your Heart, pierced by so many swords, welcome my poor soul. Receive it as the companion of your sorrows at the foot of the Cross, on which Jesus died for the redemption of the world.

With you, sorrowful Virgin, I will gladly suffer all the trials, sufferings, and afflictions that it shall please our Lord to send me. I offer them all to you in memory of your sorrows so that every thought of my mind and every beat of my heart may be an act of compassion and of love for you.

Dearest Mother, have pity on me, reconcile me to your Divine Son, Jesus, keep me in His grace, and assist me in my last agony, so that I may meet you in heaven together with your loving Son.

Hymn — Stabat Mater

AT THE Cross her station keeping,
Stood the mournful Mother weeping,
Close to Jesus to the last.
Through her Heart, His sorrow sharing,

All His bitter anguish bearing,
Lo, the piercing sword has passed!

O, how sad and sore distressed,
Was that Mother highly blessed
Of the sole-begotten One.
Christ above in torment hangs,
She beneath beholds the pangs
Of her dying glorious Son.

Is there one who would not weep
'Whelmed in miseries so deep
Christ's dear Mother to behold?
Can the human heart refrain
From partaking in the pain,
In that Mother's pain untold?

Bruised, derided, cursed, defiled,
She beheld her tender Child,
All with bloody scourges rent.
For the sins of His own nation
Saw Him hang in desolation
Till His Spirit forth He sent.

O sweet Mother! fount of love,
Touch my spirit from above,
Make my heart with yours accord.
Make me feel as you have felt.
Make my soul to glow and melt
With the love of Christ, my Lord.

Holy Mother, pierce me through.
In my heart each wound renew
Of my Savior crucified.
Let me share with you His pain,

Who for all our sins was slain,
Who for me in torments died.

Let me mingle tears with you,
Mourning Him Who mourned for me,
All the days that I may live.
By the Cross with you to stay,
There with you to weep and pray,
Is all I ask of you to give.

Virgin of all virgins blest!
Listen to my fond request:
Let me share your grief Divine.
Let me, to my latest breath,
In my body bear the death
Of your dying Son Divine.

Wounded with his every wound,
Steep my soul till it has swooned
In His very Blood away.
Be to me, O Virgin, nigh,
Lest in flames I burn and die,
In His awe-full judgment day.

Christ, when You shall call me hence,
Be Your Mother my defense,
Be Your Cross my victory.
While my body here decays,
May my soul Your goodness praise,
Safe in heaven eternally.
Amen. Alleluia.

Prayer

FATHER, it was Your Will that the compassionate Mother of Your Son should stand near the Cross on which He was glorified. Grant that Your Church, having shared in Christ's Passion, may also participate in His Resurrection. We ask this through our Lord, Jesus Christ, Your Son, Who lives and reigns with You and the Holy Spirit, God, forever and ever. Amen.

Rosary Novena

Meditation

THE Rosary is a favorite means of devotion to the Blessed Virgin Mary, recommended by the Popes over many centuries. It consists of various elements:

a) *Contemplation*, in union with Mary, of a series of Mysteries of Salvation, distributed into four cycles. These Mysteries express the joy of the Messianic times, events from Christ's Public Ministry called Mysteries of Light or Luminous Mysteries,* the suffering of Christ, and the glory of the Risen Lord that fills the Church. This contemplation by its very nature encourages practical reflection and provides norms for living.

b) *The Lord's Prayer*, which by reason of its immense value is at the basis of Christian prayer and ennobles that prayer in its various expressions.

c) The litany-like succession of the *Hail Mary*, which is made up of the Angel's greeting to the

* Suggested by Pope St. John Paul II in his Apostolic Letter of Oct. 16, 2002, entitled *The Rosary of the Virgin Mary*.

Virgin (Lk 1:28) and of Elizabeth's greeting (Lk 1:42), followed by the Church's own prayer. The continued series of Hail Marys is the special characteristic of the Rosary, and their number (200) is divided into decades attached to the individual mysteries.

d) The doxology *Glory be to the Father* concludes the prayer with the glorifying of God Who is One and Three, from Whom, through Whom, and in Whom all things have their being (cf. Rom 11:36).

In her sixth and last apparition at Fatima, October 13, 1917, the Blessed Virgin insisted on the recitation of the Rosary as a powerful means for the conversion of Russia and for peace in the world. When Lucy asked, "Who are you and what do you want?" Our Lady replied: "I am the Lady of the Rosary, and I have come to warn the faithful to amend their lives and ask pardon for their sins. They must not continue to offend our Lord Who is already so deeply offended. They must say the Rosary."

Through the prayer of the Rosary untold blessings have been showered down upon all humankind throughout the ages. Through the Rosary today as in past times of peril that have threatened civilization, Mary has again come to save all humankind from the evils that overwhelm us.

But the Rosary is especially most helpful in bringing back home life to its full splendor, by raising the family to a higher family circle where God is Father and Mary is Mother and we are all children of God. The Family Rosary is a practical way to strengthen the unity of family life.

The Word of God

"Who is this that comes forth like the dawn, beautiful as the moon, bright as the sun, formidable as an army with banners?" *—Song 6:10*

"Listen to me, my faithful children, and blossom, like a rose planted by a stream of water. Send out your fragrance like incense, and bring forth blossoms like a lily; scatter your fragrance and sing a hymn of praise, blessing the Lord for everything he has done."

—Sir 39:13-14

Novena Prayers

Novena Prayer

MY DEAREST Mother Mary, behold me, your child, in prayer at your feet. Accept this Holy Rosary, which I offer you in accordance with your requests at Fatima, as a proof of my tender love for you, for the intentions of the Sacred Heart of Jesus, in atonement for the offenses committed against your Immaculate Heart, and for this special favor that I earnestly request in my Rosary Novena. *(Mention your request.)*

I beg you to present my petition to your Divine Son. If you will pray for me, I cannot be refused. I know, dearest Mother, that you want me to seek God's holy Will concerning my request.

If what I ask for should not be granted, pray that I may receive that which will be of greater benefit to my soul.

I offer you this spiritual "Bouquet of Roses" because I love you. I put all my confidence in you, since your prayers before God are most powerful. For the greater glory of God and for the sake of Jesus, your loving Son, hear and grant my prayer. Sweet Heart of Mary, be my salvation.

THE HOLY ROSARY

See Prayer before the Rosary on page 69.

ON THE Cross: In the Name of the Father, etc. I believe in God, the Father Almighty, Creator of heaven and earth, and in Jesus Christ, His only Son, our Lord, Who was conceived by the Holy Spirit, born of the Virgin Mary, suffered under Pontius Pilate, was crucified, died and was buried; He descended into hell; on the third day He rose again from the dead; He ascended into heaven, and is seated at the right hand of God the Father Almighty; from there He will come to judge the living and the dead. I believe in the Holy Spirit, the holy catholic Church, the communion of saints, the forgiveness of sins, the resurrection of the body, and life everlasting. Amen.

On the first large bead: Our Father, etc.

On the next three beads: For an increase of faith, hope, and charity. Hail Mary, etc. *(3 times)*

Glory be to the Father, etc.

Fatima Prayer (after each decade): "O my Jesus, forgive us our sins, save us from the fire of hell, take all souls to heaven, and help especially those most in need of Your mercy."

See Mysteries and concluding prayers on pages 70-77.

The Immaculate Conception of the Blessed Virgin Mary

Meditation

THE Church teaches that from the first moment of her conception the Blessed Virgin Mary possessed sanctifying grace, even the fullness of grace, with the infused virtues and gifts of the Holy Spirit. Yet she remained subject to death and other pains and miseries of life that her Son Himself willed to undergo.

Mary, "at the first instant of her conception, by a singular privilege and grace of the Omnipotent God, in virtue of the merits of Jesus Christ, Savior of mankind, was preserved from all stain of original sin."

This article of faith is founded upon Scripture and upon the constant Tradition of the Church. Since God Himself had announced from the beginning of the world that Mary was destined "to crush the head" of the infernal serpent through her Divine Son, she could not have begun her life by being wounded herself by his poisonous bite and subject to his power. The Archangel Gabriel called her "full of grace" because she never was deprived of sanctifying grace, and consequently she possessed this grace in the first moment of her conception.

The Fathers and writers of the Church compare Mary to the ark of Noah that alone escaped the universal deluge; to the thornbush which Moses saw burning, but not consumed; to the enclosed garden; to the rod of Aaron which, when laid in the ark, budded and blossomed without having taken root; to the fleece of Gideon that remained dry while the ground all around it became moist with dew. They look upon Mary as the Queen who came from the Most High, perfect, beautiful, and without original sin; as the paradise of innocence that God Himself planted and protected against all the attacks of the poisonous serpent.

Reason, too, approves of Mary's Immaculate Conception, for this privilege corresponds with her sublime vocation. She was the throne of God, the wonderful palace in which the Son of God chose to dwell for nine months. Her womb was the chosen place honored by the mysterious working of the Holy Spirit. If everything that comes in contact with God must be pure and immaculate, purity was necessary for her, the vessel in which the Son of God formed His Flesh and Blood. Her Immaculate Conception is a brilliant witness to the sanctity of Jesus, her Son.

If Jesus, the Son of God, could choose for His Mother her who pleased Him most, He would surely choose one acceptable to the Blessed Trinity and worthy of the great honor for which she was destined. Mary was, therefore not only free from all actual sin, but she also remained exempt from original sin; otherwise, she would not have been a Mother suitable for Jesus Christ, the Son of God.

As Eve received natural life from Adam, Mary received spiritual life, the life of grace, through her Son. If Eve was originally immaculate, Mary, who is superior to Eve in merits, could not be inferior to her in dignity. Since Eve was immaculate in her formation, Mary must have been immaculate in her conception.

God Himself has testified to Mary's Immaculate Conception by miracles. Who can number the wonders that have been wrought at Lourdes, where she appeared eighteen times and declared to Bernadette and to the world: "I am the Immaculate Conception," just four years after this doctrine was defined as a dogma of faith? Mary declared to the whole world her approval of this doctrine and that she was not only immaculately conceived, but that she is the Immaculate Conception.

We should be grateful to God for the grace of Baptism by which we were cleansed from original sin and spiritually regenerated and sanctified. We ought to ask the Immaculate Virgin Mary to guard us against every sin, above all against every mortal sin, lest we lose the grace of

God, infinitely greater than all the riches of the world.

The Solemnity of the Immaculate Conception, a Holyday of Obligation, is celebrated on December 8. The Immaculate Conception is honored also on the feast of Our Lady of Lourdes, February 11, and in the devotion of the Miraculous Medal.

The Word of God

"You are the glory of Jerusalem, the surpassing pride of Israel, the great honor of our people. . . . May you be blessed by the LORD Almighty forever and ever."

—Jud 15:9, 10

"I rejoice in the LORD with all my heart; my soul exults in my God. For he has clothed me in garments of salvation and wrapped me in a robe of saving justice, like . . . a bride bedecked with her jewels." *—Isa 61:10*

"A great sign appeared in heaven: a woman clothed with the sun, with the moon beneath her feet, and a crown of twelve stars on her head." *—Rev 12:1*

Novena Prayers

Novena Prayer

IMMACULATE Virgin Mary, you were pleasing in the sight of God from the first moment of your conception in the womb of your mother, St. Anne. You were chosen to be the Mother of Jesus Christ, the Son of God. I believe the teaching of Holy Mother the Church, that "at the first instant of [your] conception, by the singular privilege and grace of Almighty God, in virtue of the merits of Jesus Christ, Savior of mankind" and your beloved Son, you were "preserved from all stain of original sin." I thank God for this wonderful privilege and grace He bestowed upon you as I honor your Immaculate Conception.

Look graciously upon me as I implore this special favor. *(Mention your request.)*

Virgin Immaculate, Mother of God and my Mother, from your throne in heaven, turn your eyes of pity upon me. Filled with confidence in your goodness and power, I beg you to help me in this journey of life, which is so full of dangers for my soul. I entrust myself entirely to you, that I may never be the slave of the devil through sin, but may always live a humble and pure life. I consecrate myself to you forever, for my only desire is to love your Divine Son Jesus.

Mary, since none of your devout servants has ever perished, may I, too, be saved. Amen.

A Prayer of Saint Ephrem

BLESSED Virgin, immaculate and pure, you are the sinless Mother of your Son, Who is the mighty Lord of the universe. Since you are holy and inviolate, the hope of the hopeless and sinful, I sing your praises. I praise you as full of every grace, for you bore the God-Man. I venerate you; I invoke you and implore your aid.

Holy and Immaculate Virgin, help me in every need that presses upon me and free me from all the temptations of the devil. Be my intercessor and advocate at the hour of death and judgment. Deliver me from the fire that is not extinguished and from the outer darkness.

Make me worthy of the glory of your Son, O dearest and most kind Virgin Mother. You indeed are my most secure and only hope, for you are holy in the sight of God, to whom be honor and glory, majesty and power forever. Amen.

Prayer

FATHER, You prepared the Virgin Mary to be the worthy Mother of Your Son. You made it possible for her to share beforehand in the salvation Your Son, Jesus Christ, would bring by His Death, and kept her without sin from the first moment of her conception. Give us the grace by her prayers ever to live in Your presence without sin. We ask this through the same Christ our Lord. Amen.

The Miraculous Medal

Meditation

THE medal of the Immaculate Conception, commonly called the Miraculous Medal, was manifested to a spiritual daughter of Saint Vincent de Paul, Saint Catherine Labouré. This took place in the chapel of the Motherhouse of the Sisters of Charity, 140 rue du Bac, Paris, France.

Sister Catherine, during her novitiate days, received extraordinary favors from God, such as visions of the heart of Saint Vincent and manifestations of our Lord in the Blessed Sacrament. In 1830 she was blessed with the apparitions of Mary Immaculate to which we owe the Miraculous Medal.

Saint Catherine describes the apparition of our Lady on November 27, 1830, in these words: "Her feet rested on a white globe. I saw rings on her fingers, and each ring was set with gems. The larger gems emitted greater rays and the smaller gems, smaller rays. I could not express what I saw, the beauty and the brilliance of the dazzling rays. A voice said, 'They are the symbols of the graces I shed upon those who ask for them.'

"A frame formed round the Blessed Virgin. Within it was written in letters of gold: 'O Mary, conceived without sin, pray for us who have recourse to you.' Then the voice said, 'Have a Medal struck after this model. All who wear it will receive great graces; they should wear it around the neck.' At this instant the tableau seemed to turn, and I beheld the reverse of the Medal: a large 'M' surmounted by a bar and a cross; beneath the 'M' were the Hearts of Jesus and Mary, the one crowned with thorns, the other pierced with a sword."

When Saint Catherine related the vision to her confessor, he asked her whether she had seen any writing on the back of the Medal. She answered that she had seen none at all. He told her to ask the Blessed Virgin what to put there. The Sister prayed to Mary a long time and one day during meditation she seemed to hear a voice saying, "The 'M' and the two hearts express enough."

The Medal was made according to our Lady's design. It was freely circulated and in a short time was worn by millions. Many graces were given and blessings bestowed until the little Medal of the Immaculate Conception became known by the name it bears today, the Miraculous Medal.

The Word of God

"All the words of my mouth are upright. . . . All of them are clear to those who are intelligent and right to those who have acquired knowledge. Choose my instruction rather than silver and knowledge instead of pure gold." *—Prov 8:8-10*

"I love those who love me, and those who diligently seek me will find me. With me are riches and honor, enduring wealth and prosperity. My fruit is better than the finest gold, and what I yield surpasses pure silver." *—Prov 8:17-19*

". . . listen to me; blessed are those who keep my ways. Listen to instruction and gain wisdom; do not reject it." *—Prov 8:32-33*

Novena Prayers

Opening Prayer

COME, Holy Spirit, fill the hearts of Your faithful, and kindle in them the fire of Your love. Send forth Your Spirit, and they shall be created; and You shall renew the face of the earth.

O God, You instructed the hearts of the faithful by the light of the Holy Spirit. Grant us in the same Spirit to be truly wise and ever to rejoice in His consolation, through Jesus Christ our Lord. Amen.

O Mary, conceived without sin, pray for us who have recourse to you. *(3 times)*

Lord Jesus Christ, You have been pleased to glorify by numberless miracles the Blessed Virgin Mary, immaculate from the first moment of her conception. Grant that all who devoutly implore her protection on earth may eternally enjoy Your presence in heaven, Who, with the Father and the Holy Spirit, live and reign, God, forever and ever. Amen.

Lord Jesus Christ, for the accomplishment of Your works, You have chosen the weak things of the world, that no flesh may glory in Your sight. And for a better and more widely diffused belief in the Immaculate Conception of Your Mother, You have wished that the Miraculous Medal be manifested to Saint Catherine Labouré. Grant, we beseech You, that filled with like humility, we may glorify this mystery by word and work. Amen.

Memorare

REMEMBER, O most gracious Virgin Mary, that never was it known that anyone who fled to your protection, implored your help, or sought your intercession, was left unaided. Inspired with this confidence, I fly to you, O Virgin of virgins, my Mother. To you I come, before you I stand, sinful and sorrowful. O Mother of the Word Incarnate, despise not my petitions, but in your mercy hear and answer me. Amen.

Novena Prayer

IMMACULATE Virgin Mary, Mother of our Lord Jesus Christ and our Mother, penetrated with the most lively confidence in your all-powerful and never-failing intercession, manifested so often through the Miraculous Medal, we your loving and trustful children implore you to obtain for us the graces and favors we ask during this Novena, if they be beneficial to our immortal souls, and the souls for which we pray. *(Mention your request.)*

You know, Mary, how often our souls have been the sanctuaries of your Son Who hates iniquity. Obtain for us then a deep hatred of sin and that purity of heart which will attach us to God alone so that our every thought, word, and deed may tend to His greater glory.

Obtain for us also a spirit of prayer and self-denial that we may recover by penance what we have lost by sin and at length attain to that blessed abode where you are the Queen of Angels and of people. Amen.

Act of Consecration

VIRGIN Mother of God, Mary Immaculate, we dedicate and consecrate ourselves to you under the title of Our Lady of the Miraculous Medal. May this Medal be a sure sign of your affection for us and a constant reminder of our duties toward you. Ever while wearing it, may we be blessed by your loving protection and preserved in the grace of your Son.

Most powerful Virgin, Mother of our Savior, keep us close to you every moment of our lives. Obtain for us, your children, the grace of a happy death; so that, in union with you, we may enjoy the blessing of heaven forever. Amen.

Mary, conceived without sin, pray for us who have recourse to you. *(3 times)*

Our Lady of Guadalupe

Meditation

ACCORDING to tradition, the Blessed Virgin appeared to a fifty-five-year-old Aztec Indian, Juan Diego, who was hurrying to Mass in Mexico City, on Saturday, December 9, 1531. She sent him to Bishop Zumaraga to ask that a church be built on the spot where she stood. She was at the same place that evening and Sunday evening to get the Bishop's answer. After cross-questioning Juan, the Bishop ordered him to ask for a sign from the lady who had said she was the Mother of God.

Mary spoke to Juan in these words: "Know and take heed, my dear little son, that I am the holy Mary, ever Virgin, Mother of the true God for Whom we live, the Creator of all the world, Maker of heaven and earth. I urgently desire that a church should be built here, to bear witness to my love, my compassion, my help and protection, for I am a merciful Mother to you and to all your people who love me and trust in me and invoke my help."

Our Lady would give the Bishop a sign. She told Juan to go up to the rocks and gather roses. He knew it was neither the time nor the place for roses, but he obeyed. Gathering the roses into the long cloak worn by Mexican Indians, he returned to the Blessed Mother who arranged them. When he arrived at the Bishop's home, Juan unfolded his cloak and the roses fell out. Startled to see the Bishop and his attendants kneeling before him, he looked at the cloak and saw there the figure of the Virgin Mary, just as he had described her. The picture was venerated in the Bishop's chapel and soon after carried in procession to the first church.

The picture that has aroused all this devotion is a representation of the Immaculate Conception, with the sun, moon, and stars, according to the text in the Book of Revelation. Mary, clothed in a blue robe dotted with stars, stands on the crescent moon. Underneath the crescent is a supporting Angel. The rays of the sun shoot out on all sides from behind the Blessed Mother.

In 1709, a rich and beautiful shrine was erected near Mexico City; in 1904, it was made a basilica and contains the picture. Pilgrimages have been made to this shrine almost uninterruptedly since 1531. A much larger New Basilica was opened in 1976. Twenty Popes favored the shrine and its tradition.

The apparition of Our Lady of Guadalupe is Mary's only recorded appearance in North America. Pope Pius XII said, "We are certain that so long as you—Our Lady of Guadalupe—are recognized as Queen and Mother, America and Mexico are saved." He proclaimed her the Patroness of the Americas. The United States was dedicated to the Immaculate Conception by the Third Plenary Council of Baltimore in 1846.

The image of Our Lady of Guadalupe is the image of the Immaculate Conception. As patroness of Pan-American unity, Our Lady of Guadalupe influences her children to turn toward one another in common love for her and her beloved Son. Because of the close link between the Church in Mexico and the Church in the United States, this feast is also celebrated in the United States on December 12.

The Word of God

"I have chosen and consecrated this house so that my name may be there forever and my eyes and my heart shall constantly be there." *—2 Chr 7:16*

"You are beautiful . . . , my beloved, as lovely as Jerusalem, as majestic as an army with banners." *—Song 6:4*

"Who is this that comes forth like the dawn, beautiful as the moon, bright as the sun, formidable as an army with banners?" *—Song 6:10*

Novena Prayers

Novena Prayer

OUR Lady of Guadalupe, according to your message in Mexico I venerate you as "the Virgin Mother of the true God for Whom we live, the Creator of all the world, Maker of heaven and earth." In spirit I kneel before your most holy Image which you miraculously imprinted upon the cloak of the Indian Juan Diego, and with the faith of the countless numbers of pilgrims who visit your shrine, I beg you for this favor. *(Mention your request.)*

Remember, O Immaculate Virgin, the words you spoke to your devout client, "I am a merciful Mother to you and to all your people who love me and trust in me and invoke my help. I listen to their lamentations and solace all their sorrows and their sufferings." I beg you to be a

THE HOLY ROSARY

PRAYER BEFORE THE ROSARY

QUEEN of the Holy Rosary, you have deigned to come to Fatima to reveal to the three shepherd children the treasures of grace hidden in the Rosary. Inspire my heart with a sincere love of this devotion, in order that by meditating on the Mysteries of our Redemption which are recalled in it, I may be enriched with its fruits and obtain peace for the world, the conversion of sinners, and the favor which I ask of you in this Rosary. *(Here mention your request.)* I ask it for the greater glory of God, for your own honor, and for the good of souls, especially for my own. Amen.

The Five Joyful Mysteries

Said on Mondays and Saturdays [except during Lent], and the Sundays from Advent to Lent.

1. The Annunciation
For the love of humility.

2. The Visitation
For charity toward my neighbor.

3. The Nativity
For the spirit of poverty.

4. The Presentation
For the virtue of obedience.

5. Finding in the Temple
For the virtue of piety.

The Five Luminous Mysteries

Said on Thursdays [except during Lent].

1. The Baptism of Jesus
For living my Baptismal Promises.

2. Christ's Self-Manifestation at Cana
For doing whatever Jesus says.

3. Proclamation of the Kingdom
For seeking God's forgiveness.

4. The Transfiguration
Becoming a New Person in Christ.

5. Institution of the Eucharist
For active participation at Mass.

The Five Sorrowful Mysteries

Said on Tuesdays and Fridays throughout the year, and every day from Ash Wednesday until Easter.

1. Agony in the Garden
For true contrition.

2. Scourging at the Pillar
For the virtue of purity.

3. Crowning with Thorns
For moral courage.

4. Carrying of the Cross
For the virtue of patience.

5. The Crucifixion
For final perseverance.

The Five Glorious Mysteries

Said on Wednesdays [except during Lent], and the Sundays from Easter to Advent.

1. The Resurrection
For the virtue of faith.

2. The Ascension
For the virtue of hope.

3. Descent of the Holy Spirit
For love of God.

4. Assumption of the B.V.M.
For devotion to Mary.

5. Crowning of the B.V.M.
For eternal happiness.

PRAYER AFTER THE ROSARY

O GOD, Whose only-begotten Son, by His Life, Death, and Resurrection, has purchased for us the rewards of eternal life; grant, we beseech You, that, meditating upon these Mysteries of the Most Holy Rosary of the Blessed Virgin Mary, we may imitate what they contain and obtain what they promise, through the same Christ our Lord. Amen.

℣. May the divine assistance remain always with us. ℟. Amen.

℣. And may the souls of the faithful departed, through the mercy of God, rest in peace. ℟. Amen.

THE LUMINOUS MYSTERIES

THESE Mysteries, i.e., Mysteries of Light or the Luminous Mysteries, suggested by Pope John Paul II, are intended to offer contemplation on important parts of Christ's Public Life in addition to the contemplation on His Childhood, His Sufferings, and His Risen Life offered by the traditional Mysteries.

The Pope assigned these Mysteries to Thursday while transferring the Joyful Mysteries—normally said on that day—to Saturday because of the special Marian presence in them.

merciful Mother to me, because I sincerely love you and trust in you and invoke your help.

I entreat you, Our Lady of Guadalupe, to grant my request, if this should be the Will of God, in order that I may "bear witness to your love, your compassion, your help and protection." Do not forsake me in my needs.

Our Lady of Guadalupe, pray for us.

3 Hail Marys

Prayer by Pope St. John Paul II

O IMMACULATE Virgin, Mother of the true God and Mother of the Church! You, who from this place reveal your clemency and your pity to all those who ask for your protection; hear the prayer that we address to you with filial trust, and present it to your Son, Jesus, our sole Redeemer.

Mother of Mercy, Teacher of hidden and silent sacrifice, to you, who come to meet us sinners, we dedicate on this day all our being and all our love. We also dedicate to you our life, our work, our joys, our infirmities, and our sorrows.

Grant peace, justice, and prosperity to our people, for we entrust to your care all that we have and all that we are, Our Lady and Mother.

We wish to be entirely yours and to walk with you along the way of complete faithfulness to Jesus Christ in His Church: hold us always with your loving hand.

Virgin of Guadalupe, Mother of the Americas, we pray to you for all the Bishops, that they may lead the faithful along paths of intense Christian life, of love and humble service of God and souls.

Contemplate this immense harvest, and intercede with the Lord that He may instill a hunger for holiness in the whole People of God, and grant abundant vocations of priests and religious, strong in the faith and zealous dispensers of God's mysteries.

Grant to our homes the grace of loving and respecting life in its beginnings, with the same love with which you conceived in your womb the life of the Son of God.

Blessed Virgin Mary, Mother of Fair Love, protect our families, so that they may always be united, and bless the upbringing of our children.

Our Hope, look upon us with compassion, teach us to go continually to Jesus and, if we fall, help us to rise again, to return to Him, by means of the confession of our faults and sins in the Sacrament of Penance, which gives peace to the soul. We beg you to grant us a great love for all the holy Sacraments, which are, as it were, the signs that your Son left us on earth.

Thus, Most Holy Mother, with the peace of God in our conscience, with our hearts free from evil and hatred, we will be able to bring to all true joy and true peace, which come to us from your Son, our Lord Jesus Christ, Who with God the Father and the Holy Spirit, lives and reigns forever. Amen. *Mexico, January 1979*

Prayer

GOD of power and mercy, You blessed the Americas at Tepeyac with the presence of the Virgin Mary at Guadalupe. May her prayers help all men and women to accept each other as brothers and sisters. Through Your justice present in our hearts, may Your peace reign in the world. We ask this through our Lord Jesus Christ, Your Son, Who lives and reigns with You and the Holy Spirit, God, forever and ever. Amen.

Glory Be
Glory Be
4th Mystery and Our Father
3rd Mystery and Our Father
10 Hail Marys
10 Hail Marys
Glory Be
2nd Mystery and Our Father
5th Mystery and Our Father
Glory Be
10 Hail Marys
10 Hail Marys
Glory Be
Hail! Holy Queen
1st Mystery and Our Father
Glory Be
3 Hail Marys
1 Our Father
Sign of the Cross and Apostles' Creed

DEVOTIONS

The Holy Rosary

Prayer before the Rosary

QUEEN of the Holy Rosary, you have deigned to come to Fatima to reveal to the three shepherd children the treasures of grace hidden in the Rosary. Inspire my heart with a sincere love of this devotion, in order that by meditating on the Mysteries of our Redemption which are recalled in it, I may be enriched with its fruits and obtain peace for the world, the conversion of sinners and of Russia, and the favor which I ask of you in this Rosary. *(Mention your request.)* I ask it for the greater glory of God, for your own honor, and for the good of souls, especially for my own. Amen.

The Five Joyful Mysteries

Said on Mondays and Saturdays [except during Lent], and the Sundays from Advent to Lent.

3. The Nativity
For the spirit of poverty.

1. The Annunciation
For the love of humility.

4. The Presentation
For the virtue of obedience.

2. The Visitation
For charity toward my neighbor.

5. Finding in the Temple
For the virtue of piety.

The Five Luminous Mysteries *

Said on Thursdays [except during Lent].

*Added to the Mysteries of the Rosary by Pope St. John Paul II in his Apostolic Letter of October 16, 2002, entitled ***The Rosary of the Virgin Mary.***

1. The Baptism of Jesus
For living my Baptismal Promises.

2. The Wedding at Cana
For doing whatever Jesus says.

3. Proclamation of the Kingdom
For seeking God's forgiveness.

4. The Transfiguration
Becoming a New Person in Christ.

5. Institution of the Eucharist
For active participation at Mass.

The Five Sorrowful Mysteries

Said on Tuesdays and Fridays throughout the year, and every day from Ash Wednesday until Easter.

1. Agony in the Garden
For true contrition.

2. Scourging at the Pillar
For the virtue of purity.

3. Crowning with Thorns
For moral courage.

4. Carrying of the Cross
For the virtue of patience.

5. The Crucifixion
For final perseverance.

The Five Glorious Mysteries

Said on Wednesdays [except during Lent], and the Sundays from Easter to Advent.

1. The Resurrection
For the virtue of faith.

2. The Ascension
For the virtue of hope.

3. Descent of the Holy Spirit
For love of God.

4. Assumption of the BVM
For devotion to Mary.

5. Crowning of the BVM
For eternal happiness.

The Hail! Holy Queen

HAIL! Holy Queen, Mother of Mercy, our life, our sweetness, and our hope. To you do we cry, poor banished children of Eve. To you do we send up our sighs, mourning and weeping in this valley of tears. Turn then, O most gracious advocate, your eyes of mercy toward us; and after this, our exile, show unto us the blessed fruit of your womb, Jesus. O clement! O loving! O sweet Virgin Mary!

℣. Pray for us, O Holy Mother of God.

℟. That we may be made worthy of the promises of Christ.

Prayer after the Rosary

O GOD, Whose Only Begotten Son, by His Life, Death, and Resurrection, has purchased for us the rewards of eternal life; grant, we beseech You, that, meditating upon these Mysteries of the Most Holy Rosary of the Blessed Virgin Mary, we may imitate what they contain and obtain what they promise, through the same Christ our Lord. Amen.

℣. May the Divine assistance remain always with us.

℟. Amen.

℣. And may the souls of the faithful departed, through the mercy of God, rest in peace.

℟. Amen.

The Litany of Loreto

LORD, have mercy.
Christ, have mercy.
Lord, have mercy.
Christ, hear us.
Christ, graciously hear us.
God, the Father of heaven,
have mercy on us.
God, the Son, Redeemer of the world,
have mercy on us.
God, the Holy Spirit,
have mercy on us.
Holy Trinity, one God,
have mercy on us.
Holy Mary, *pray for us.**
Holy Mother of God,
Holy Virgin of virgins,
Mother of Christ,
Mother of the Church,
Mother of Mercy,
Mother of Divine grace,
Mother of hope,
Mother most pure,
Mother most chaste,
Mother inviolate,
Mother undefiled,
Mother most amiable,
Mother most admirable,
Mother of good counsel,

* *Pray for us* is repeated after each invocation.

Mother of our Creator,
Mother of our Savior,
Virgin most prudent,
Virgin most venerable,
Virgin most renowned,
Virgin most powerful,
Virgin most merciful,
Virgin most faithful,
Mirror of justice,
Seat of wisdom,
Cause of our joy,
Spiritual vessel,
Vessel of honor,
Singular vessel of devotion,
Mystical rose,
Tower of David,
Tower of ivory,
House of gold,
Ark of the covenant,
Gate of heaven,
Morning star,
Health of the sick,
Refuge of sinners,
Solace of migrants,
Comforter of the afflicted,
Help of Christians,
Queen of Angels,
Queen of Patriarchs,
Queen of Prophets,
Queen of Apostles,
Queen of Martyrs,

Queen of confessors,
Queen of virgins,
Queen of all Saints,
Queen conceived without original sin,
Queen Assumed into Heaven,
Queen of the Most Holy Rosary,
Queen of families,
Queen of peace,
Lamb of God, You take away the sins of the world; *spare us, O Lord!*
Lamb of God, You take away the sins of the world; *graciously hear us, O Lord!*
Lamb of God, You take away the sins of the world; *have mercy on us.*

℣. Pray for us, O holy Mother of God.

℟. That we may be made worthy of the promises of Christ.

Let us pray.
Grant, we beg You, O Lord God,
that we Your servants
may enjoy lasting health of mind and body,
and by the glorious intercession
of the Blessed Mary, ever Virgin,
be delivered from present sorrow
and enter into the joy of eternal happiness.
Through Christ our Lord.
℟. Amen.

The Five First Saturdays in Honor of the Immaculate Heart of Mary

Mary's Great Promise at Fatima

The observance of the First Saturday in honor of the Immaculate Heart of Mary is intended to console her Immaculate Heart, and to make reparation to it for all the blasphemies and ingratitude of human beings.

This devotion and the wonderful promises connected with it were revealed by the Blessed Virgin with these words recorded by Lucy, one of the three children to whom the Blessed Virgin appeared at Fatima, Portugal, in 1917:

I PROMISE to help at the hour of death, with the graces needed for salvation, whoever on the First Saturday of five consecutive months shall:

1. ***Confess and receive Holy Communion.***
2. ***Recite five decades of the Rosary.***
3. ***And keep me company for fifteen minutes while meditating on the fifteen Mysteries of the Rosary, with the intention of making reparation to me.***

In 1930, the Lord revealed to Sister Lúcia the reason why there are Five First Saturdays. There are five principal offenses against the Immaculate Heart for which reparation must be made:

1. Denial of the Immaculate Conception of Mary;
2. Denial of the perpetual virginity of Mary;
3. Denial that Mary is the spiritual Mother of all people in addition to being the Mother of Jesus;

4. Sowing in the minds of children a disrespect or hatred for Mary and her Immaculate Heart;
5. Disrespect for, or defacement of, holy images of the Blessed Virgin.

Act of Reparation

O MOST holy Virgin and our Mother,
we listen with grief to the complaints
of your Immaculate Heart surrounded with the thorns
placed therein at every moment
by the blasphemies and ingratitude
of ungrateful humanity.
We are moved by the ardent desire
of loving you as our Mother
and of promoting a true devotion
to your Immaculate Heart.

We therefore kneel before you
to manifest the sorrow we feel for the grievances
that people cause you,
and to atone by our prayers and sacrifices
for the offenses with which they return your love.
Obtain for them and for us the pardon of so many sins.
Hasten the conversion of sinners
that they may love Jesus
and cease to offend the Lord, already so much offended,
and will not fall into hell.

Turn your eyes of mercy toward us,
that we may love God with all our heart on earth
and enjoy Him forever in heaven.

The Thirty Days' Prayer to the Blessed Virgin Mary

EVER glorious and blessed Mary,
Queen of Virgins,
Mother of Mercy,
and Hope of dejected and desolate souls,
through the sword of sorrow
that pierced your Heart
while your only Son, Jesus, our Lord,
suffered death and ignominy on the Cross
and through that filial love He had for you,
grieving in your grief,
while He entrusted you to St. John,
I beg you:
take pity on my poverty and necessities,
have compassion on my anxieties and cares,
assist and comfort me in all my infirmities and miseries.
You are the sweet Consolatrix and Refuge
of the needy and the afflicted;
hear my prayer.

In just punishment for my sins,
I am encompassed with evils
and oppressed with anguish of spirit.
To whom can I flee for more secure shelter,
O loving Mother of my Lord and Savior,

except to your Motherly protection?
Listen, then, to my humble and earnest request.

I ask it
through the infinite mercy of your dear Son,
through that love and condescension
with which He embraced our nature
when in compliance with the Divine Will
you consented to conceive
and nine months later brought Him forth
to visit this world and bless it with His presence.

I ask it through that anguish of mind
with which your beloved Son was overwhelmed in the Garden
when He besought His eternal Father
to remove from Him,
if possible, the bitter chalice of His Passion.

I ask it
through the threefold repetition of His prayer in the Garden,
from which you afterward accompanied Him in sorrow
to the doleful theater of His Sufferings and Death.

I ask it
through the welts and sores of His virginal flesh,
occasioned by the cords and whips
with which He was bound and scourged,
when stripped of His seamless garment,
for which His executioners afterward cast lots.

I ask it
through the scoffs and ignominies
by which He was insulted,
the false accusations and unjust sentence
by which He was condemned to death,
and which He bore with heavenly patience.

I ask it
through His bitter tears and bloody sweat,
His silence and resignation,
His sadness and grief of Heart.

I ask it
through the Blood that trickled
from His royal and sacred Head
when struck with a scepter of a reed
and pierced with the crown of thorns.

I ask it
through the excruciating torments He suffered
when His Hands and Feet were fastened with nails
to the tree of the Cross.

I ask it
through His vehement thirst
and the bitter potion of vinegar and gall.

I ask it
through His dereliction on the Cross
when He exclaimed:
"My God, My God, why have You forsaken Me?"

I ask it
through His mercy extended to the good thief

and through His recommending His precious Soul and Spirit
into the hands of His eternal Father
before He expired, saying:
"It is consummated."

I ask it
through the Blood mixed with water,
which issued from His sacred Side,
when pierced with a lance
and from which a flood of grace has flowed to us.

I ask it
through His immaculate Life, bitter Passion,
and ignominious Death on the Cross
at which Nature itself was thrown into convulsions
by the bursting of rocks,
the rending of the Temple veil,
the earthquake,
and the darkening of the sun and moon.

I ask it
through His Descent into hell,
where He comforted the Saints of the Old Law
with His presence
and led captivity captive.

I ask it
through His glorious victory over death
when He rose again to life on the third day
and through the joy
that His appearance for forty days afterward
gave you and His Apostles and disciples

when He miraculously ascended into heaven
in your presence.

I ask it
through the grace of the Holy Spirit,
infused into the hearts of the disciples,
when He descended upon them
in the form of fiery tongues
and by which they were inspired with zeal
in the conversion of the world
when they went to preach the Gospel.

I ask it
through the awesome appearance of your Son at the last day,
when He shall come to judge the living and the dead.

I ask it
through the compassion He bore you in this life
and the ineffable joy you felt
at your Assumption into heaven,
where you are eternally absorbed
in the sweet contemplation
of His Divine perfections.

O glorious and ever-blessed Virgin,
comfort the heart of your suppliant,
by obtaining for me the grant of the intentions
that I now earnestly solicit.
(Here mention your request.)
Since I firmly believe
that my Divine Savior honors you as His beloved Mother,

to whom He can refuse nothing,
let me speedily experience the efficacy
of your powerful intercession
according to the tenderness of your Motherly affection
and according to His filial, loving Heart,
which mercifully grants the requests
and complies with the desires
of those who love and fear Him.

O most blessed Virgin,
obtain for me also from your dear Son,
our Lord and God,
a lively faith, firm hope, perfect love,
true contrition of heart,
unfeigned tears of compunction,
sincere confession,
condign satisfaction,
abstinence from sin,
love of God and neighbor,
patient bearing of affronts and ignominies,
and an opprobrious death itself
out of love for your Son,
our Savior Jesus Christ.

O sacred Mother of God,
also obtain for me
perseverance in good works,
performance of good resolutions,
mortifications of self-will,
a pious conversation through life,
and at my last moments
strong and sincere repentance

accompanied by such a lively and attentive presence of mind
as may enable me to receive
the Last Sacraments of the Church worthily
and to die in your friendship and favor.

Finally, I beg you,
obtain life everlasting for the souls
of my parents, my brothers and sisters,
and my relatives and benefactors,
living or dead.

Act of Consecration

O MARY,
Virgin most powerful and Mother of Mercy,
Queen of Heaven and Refuge of sinners,
I consecrate myself to your Immaculate Heart.

I consecrate to you my very being and my whole life:
all that I have,
all that I love,
all that I am.
I give you my body, heart, and soul,
my home, family, and country.
I desire that everything in and around me
may belong to you
and share in the benefits of your Motherly blessing.

In order that this act of consecration
may be truly efficacious and lasting,
I today renew at your feet

the promises made at my Baptism and First Communion.
I pledge that I will courageously and unceasingly profess
the truths of the holy Faith,
and live as befits a Catholic who is duly submissive
to the direction of the Pope
and the Bishops who are in communion with him.

I pledge myself to keep
the commandments of God and the Church,
in particular to keep holy the Lord's day.
I also pledge myself
to make consoling practices of the Christian religion,
especially Holy Communion,
an integral part of my life,
insofar as I shall be able to do so.
Finally, I promise you,
O glorious Mother of God
and loving Mother of all human beings,
to dedicate myself with all my heart
to the service of devotion to you.
Through the sovereignty of your Immaculate Heart,
may I thus hasten and assure the coming
of the Kingdom of the Sacred Heart
of your adorable Son
in my own heart as well as those of all people,
in my own country as well as in the whole world,
on earth as in heaven.

Our Lady of Czestochowa subtly points to her Son, Jesus, Who extends His right hand in blessing.

PRAYERS IN HONOR OF OUR LADY'S TITLES

Our Lady of Czestochowa

O MOTHER of God, Immaculate Mary,
to you do I dedicate my body and soul, all my prayers and deeds, my joys and sufferings,
all that I am and all that I have.
With a joyful heart I surrender myself to your love.
To you will I devote my services
of my own free will for the salvation of mankind
and for the help of the Holy Church
whose Mother you are.
From now on my only desire is to do
all things with you, through you, and for you.
I know I can accomplish nothing
by my own strength,
whereas you can do everything
that is the Will of your Son, Our Lord Jesus Christ.
You are always victorious.
Grant, therefore, O Helper of the faithful,
that my family, my parish, and my country
might become in truth the Kingdom
where you reign in the glorious presence of
God the Father, God the Son, and God the
Holy Spirit, forever and ever. Amen.

Our Lady of the Cenacle

MOST holy Virgin of the Cenacle,
obtain for us the gifts of the Holy Spirit.
May we live in love and perseverance
united in prayer under your guidance and teaching

for the greater glory of God.
May we labor both by word and by work
for the salvation of souls
and so deserve to enter everlasting life.
Graciously be near us,
in our present needs,
and comfort us by your power.
By your intercession
may Almighty God be pleased to grant us
the favor for which we earnestly pray.

Our Lady, Comforter of the Afflicted

IMMACULATE Mary, Mother of God,
Comforter of the Afflicted,
accept our humble and confident prayers
and aid us in our spiritual and temporal needs.
Deliver us from all evil,
especially from sin, the greatest evil.
Obtain for us from your Son
every blessing that you see we need,
both in soul and in body,
especially the blessing of Divine grace.

Comfort our souls,
which are troubled and afflicted
amid the many dangers that threaten us
and the countless miseries and misfortunes
that surround us.
Enable us to live a virtuous life,
die a holy death,
and reach eternal happiness in heaven.

Our Lady of Consolation

MARY Immaculate,
our Mother and Consolation,
with confidence I take refuge
in your most loving Heart.
You shall be the dearest object
of my love and veneration.
I shall always have recourse to you
who are the dispenser of the treasures of heaven,
that I may have peace in my sorrows,
light in my doubts,
protection in dangers,
and help in all my needs.

Be therefore my refuge, strength, and consolation,
O Mary, the Consoler.
At the hour of my death,
graciously receive the last sighs of my heart
and obtain for me a place in your heavenly home,
where all hearts will praise with one accord
the adorable Heart of Jesus
as well as your most lovable Heart forever.
Our tender Mother,
Comforter of the afflicted,
pray for us who have recourse to you.

Our Lady of Divine Providence

MARY,
Immaculate Virgin and Mother of Divine Providence,
keep my soul with the fullness of your grace.

Govern my life
and direct it in the way of virtue,
that I may fulfill the Divine Will.
Obtain for me
the pardon and remission of all my sins.
Be my refuge, my protection, my defense, and my guide
in my pilgrimage through the world.
Comfort me in the midst of trials.
Bring me safe through every danger.
Give me your sure protection in the storms of affliction.

Mary,
renew my heart spiritually,
that it may become a holy dwelling place
for your Divine Son, Jesus.
Keep far from me every kind of sin,
negligence, carelessness, cowardice, and lack of human respect.
You are the Mother of Providence
and the Virgin of pardon.
You are my hope on earth.
Grant that I may have you as my Mother
in the glory of heaven.

Our Lady of Fatima

O MOST holy Virgin Mary,
Queen of the Most Holy Rosary,
you were pleased to appear to the children of Fatima
and reveal a glorious message.

We implore you,
inspire in our hearts a fervent love
for the recitation of the Rosary.
By meditating on the mysteries of the Redemption
that are recalled therein
may we obtain the graces and virtues
that we ask,
through the merits of Jesus Christ,
our Lord and Redeemer.

Our Lady of Good Counsel

MOST glorious Virgin,
you were chosen by the eternal Counsel
to be the Mother
of the eternal Word made flesh.
You are the treasurer of Divine graces
and the advocate of sinners.
I who am your most unworthy servant
have recourse to you.
Graciously be my guide and counselor
in this valley of tears.

Obtain for me,
through the Precious Blood of your Divine Son,
the forgiveness of my sins,
the salvation of my soul,
and the means necessary to obtain it.
In like manner, obtain for holy Church
victory over her enemies
and the spread of Jesus' Kingdom
over the whole earth.

Our Lady of Guadalupe

MARY, Mother of the Americas,
your apparition at Guadalupe teaches me
that devotion to you is a source of great graces.
God has entrusted to your hands heavenly blessings.
I have but to ask for them
for the salvation of my soul.
There is nothing you want more
than to give them to me,
because you are even more anxious to save my soul
than I am,
for you know better than anyone else
the price your Son paid for it
and the precious worth of each grace
that He so graciously offers to me through you.

Let me turn to you
as a child turns to its mother in every need
and finds comfort in her glance and kind word.
For you are truly my Mother,
whose Heart is overflowing with kindness and mercy.

Our Lady of the Immaculate Conception

MARY, Virgin most pure,
your greatness began
at the first instant of your existence
with the privilege of your Immaculate Conception.
It was fitting that you should be adorned

with the greatest purity ever possible to a creature.
You are the Immaculate Virgin to whom God the Father decreed
to give His only Son.
You are the Immaculate Virgin
whom God the Son Himself chose to make His Mother.
You are the Immaculate Virgin
whom the Holy Spirit willed to make His Bride
and in whom He would work the tremendous miracle
of the Incarnation.

Help me to imitate your sinlessness
by keeping my soul free from willful sin
through the faithful observance of God's commandments.
Let me imitate your fullness of grace
by frequent reception of Communion
and assiduous prayer—
which will make my soul holy
and give me the grace I need to practice virtue.
Transform me into a living image of Jesus,
just as you were.

Our Lady of Lourdes

IMMACULATE Mary,
you appeared to St. Bernadette
and gave her a mission to build up Lourdes
as a sacred shrine to bring people to God.
Through your intercession,

countless graces have been given
to the thousands of people
who have flocked to Lourdes.
Some have even received the grace of physical healing.

I join my prayers to the pilgrims at your shrine
who sing thousands of *Aves* to you.
I place all my trust in you
and give you all my love.

Our Lady of La Salette

OUR Lady of La Salette,
true Mother of Sorrows,
remember the tears that you shed on Calvary.
Remember, also, the care that you take
to shield me from the justice of God.
Do not now abandon your child,
for whom you have done so much.

Inspired with this consoling thought,
I cast myself at your feet,
in spite of my unfaithfulness and ingratitude.
Do not reject my prayer,
O reconciling Virgin.
Convert me;
obtain for me the grace to love Jesus
above all things
and to console you by a holy life,
so that one day I may see you in heaven.

Queen of Angels, pray for us.

Mother of God, pray for us.

Our Lady, Mediatrix of Graces

MOST holy Mary,
great Queen of Heaven,
the very treasure of life
and ever-flowing channel of Divine grace!
By the ineffable virtues
infused into your soul
at your Immaculate Conception,
you were so pleasing in God's sight
that you were privileged
to conceive in your virginal womb
the very Author of life and of grace,
Jesus Christ, our Lord.
By becoming the Mother of the God-Man,
you also became the Mother of redeemed humankind.

Mother of grace and life,
of mercy and forgiveness,
turn to me your kind face.
Behold my many miseries of body and soul.
Raise me up to a state
of perfect friendship with God.
Obtain for me
the grace of final perseverance.

Our Lady, Mother of Mercy

HAIL, most gracious Mother of Mercy,
through whom we obtain forgiveness!
Who would not love you?
You are our light in uncertainty,

our comfort in sorrow,
our consolation in trial,
our refuge from every danger and temptation.
You are our sure hope of salvation,
second only to your Only Begotten Son.

Happy are they who love you,
our Lady!
I beg you to listen to my prayers,
even though I am a poor sinner.
Scatter the darkness of my sins
by the bright beams of your holiness
so that I may be pleasing to you.

Our Lady, Mother of Good Hope

MARY Immaculate,
the precious name of Mother of Good Hope,
with which we honor you,
fills our hearts to overflowing
with the sweetest consolation
and moves us to hope for every blessing from you.

If such a title has been given to you,
it is a sure sign
that no one has recourse to you in vain.

Therefore, with a mother's love
accept our devout homage,
as we earnestly beg you
to be gracious to us in our every need.

Above all, we beg you to make us live
in constant union with you

and your Divine Son Jesus on earth
so that we may deserve
to be with you in heaven.

Our Lady of Mount Carmel

MARY, Virgin most powerful,
I honor you under the title of Our Lady of Mount Carmel.
It recalls the hermits who remained in God's presence
night and day on Mount Carmel in Palestine.
Teach me also to stand always in God's presence
every moment of my life.
And to do so,
let me stay always in your presence,
calling upon your help.
Remember me in my needs,
and show yourself my Mother.

Shed upon me more and more the living light
of the flame that made you blessed.
Enkindle in me the heavenly love
with which you loved your dear Son, Jesus.
Obtain for me from Jesus
the gifts of humility, chastity, and meekness,
which were the fairest adornments of your immaculate soul.
And after my earthly pilgrimage,
grant that my soul may obtain the glory of heaven
through the merits of Christ
and your intercession.

Our Lady, Mother of Perpetual Help

O MOTHER of Perpetual Help,
grant that I may ever invoke your powerful name,
which is the safeguard of the living
and the salvation of the dying.
O pure Virgin Mary,
let your name be henceforth ever on my lips.
Whenever I call on you by name,
hasten to help me.
When I speak your sacred name
or even think of you,
what consolation and confidence,
what sweetness and emotion fill my soul!

I thank God
for having given you
so sweet, powerful, and lovely a name
for my good.
Let my love for you prompt me ever to greet you
as Mother of Perpetual Help.

Our Lady, Queen of Peace

MOST holy Virgin,
by your Divine Motherhood you merited
to share in your Divine Son's prerogative of universal Kingship,
and to be called Queen of Peace.
May your powerful intercession guard your people
from all hatred and discord among themselves
and direct their hearts in the way of peace.

Your Son came to teach us this way
for the good and well-being of all,
and your Church continues to guide our steps
along that same way.

Look kindly upon the efforts of Christ's Vicar
to call together and unite nations
around the only center of saving faith.
Enlighten the rulers of our country
and of all countries on earth
to follow this path to peace.
Grant that there may be peace
in our hearts,
in our families,
and in our world.

Our Lady of the Rosary

MARY, Queen of the Holy Rosary,
your Divine Son Jesus is the perfect Mediator
between God and human beings,
because He alone could in all justice merit
our reconciliation with God
as well as the graces that God would impart
after the reconciliation.
You are a Mediatrix in union with Christ
from Whom your mediation draws all its power.
You merited the title of Unique Associate
above all by your union with Christ
in His redemptive sacrifice.
After Jesus, no one suffered as you did.
Now your action is primarily one of intercession.
In your contemplation of God,

you behold our needs with our prayers
and you beg God to grant these favors.

May the faithful recitation of my Rosary
be a sign of my gratitude to Jesus and to you
for all you have done for me
in bringing about my Redemption.
May my Rosary also be a means
of obtaining all the graces I need
for the sanctification and salvation of my soul.

Our Lady of the Sacred Heart

O LADY of the Sacred Heart,
remember what ineffable power
your Divine Son has given you
over His own adorable Heart.
You are the heavenly Treasurer of the Heart
that is the limitless source of all graces.
You are free to open it to us
at your good pleasure
in order to pour out upon humankind
the riches of love and mercy,
light and salvation,
that are contained in it.
Graciously hear our prayers
and grant the request we now make.
(Mention your request.)

Our Lady, Mother of Sorrows

MARY, Mother of Sorrows,
your power to suffer was great on earth.
You were associated in all that Jesus did,

His sufferings as well as His joys.
On Calvary, you saw Him crucified
and received His dead body into your arms.
What sorrow this constituted for your Mother's Heart!
But we know that this suffering enabled you
to become the Mother of Life,
the Mother of supernatural life for souls.

You can now suffer no more,
but those who are left on earth still suffer.
Help me to offer all my sufferings and sorrows,
no matter how big or how little,
for the Church of God
and for the souls of all people.

Our Lady, Associate of the Redeemer

BLESSED are you, O Mary,
Virgin Mother of Christ
and the generous Associate of our Redeemer.
You conceived, bore, and nourished Christ,
you presented Him to the Father in the Temple,
and you were united with Him in His work,
especially in His Death on the Cross.
You thus cooperated,
by your obedience, faith, hope, and love,
in the work of the Savior
in giving back supernatural life to souls.

Help us to share in the Redemption
by uniting our sufferings to those of Christ.
Grant that we may even rejoice in them,

so that we may be filled with joy
when He comes again in glory.

Our Lady, Daughter of Zion

BLESSED are you, O Mary,
Daughter of Zion.
You were chosen by God
as the crown of Israel
and the beginning of the Church
to reveal to all peoples
that salvation is born from Israel
and that the new family of God
springs from a chosen root.

By nature, you are the daughter of Adam
who by your sinlessness undid Eve's sin.
By faith you are the true child of Abraham
who first believed and so conceived.
By descent you are the branch
from the root of Jesse,
bearing the flower that is Jesus.

Obtain for us
to follow your example
by offering you the homage of our heartfelt faith
and placing in you alone our hope of salvation.

Our Lady, Handmaid of the Lord

BLESSED are you, O Mary,
Handmaid of the Lord.
You welcomed the Angel's announcement
and became the Mother of the Word.
In the silence of your Heart,

you meditated on the heavenly words
and became a disciple of the Divine Master.
Open our hearts
to the blessedness of listening.
By the power of the Holy Spirit,
may we too become a holy place
in which the Word of salvation
is fulfilled today.

Our Lady, Mother of Reconciliation

BLESSED are you, O Mary,
Mother of Reconciliation.
Although you were sinless,
God gave you
a Heart of compassion for sinners
in order to call them back to His love.

Teach us to see your love as our Mother
and turn to you with trust
as we ask forgiveness from God.
Make us contemplate your beauty of spirit
and seek to turn away from sin in its ugliness.
Help us to take your words and example to heart
and learn to keep your Son's commandments.

Our Lady, Mother and Teacher

BLESSED are you, O Mary,
Mother and Teacher in the Spirit.
You are a Teacher
who keeps the words of the Lord
in her heart.
You are a Mother

who gently invites us to go up
to the mountain of the Lord,
which is Christ Himself.

As our Teacher,
instruct us in the fear of God,
to live by the spirit of the Gospel,
to look up to you in prayer,
to love God above all things,
to be rapt in contemplation of His Word,
and to serve the needs of others.
As our Mother,
watch over us
and keep us under your protection.
Make us imitate your virtues
and reach our heavenly home with you.

Our Lady, the New Woman

BLESSED are you, O Mary,
the New Woman.
Conceived without stain of sin
and enriched by gifts of grace,
you are the New Eve,
associated with Jesus, the New Adam,
as His Mother and Companion.
By your faith and obedience,
you undid the loss inflicted on humankind
by the unfaithfulness and disobedience
of the first Eve.

Help us to emulate
the active and responsible consent
that you gave in dialogue with God.

Teach us to make courageous choices
as you did in choosing the state of virginity.
Give us a love for the poor and lowly
in accord with your life and sentiments
as expressed in the *Magnificat*.

Our Lady, Queen of the Universe

BLESSED are you, O Mary,
Queen of the Universe.
You are gloriously reigning in heaven
because you were the lowly handmaid on earth.
You are our Queen and Mother
because you became the Mother
of the Messianic King.
You are the Queen who intercedes for us
with her Son
as our advocate of grace.
You are the Queen
who is the sign of the Church in future glory,
because what was accomplished in you
will be accomplished in all members
of Christ's Mystical Body.

As your Queenship is one of love and service
rather than pomp and power,
teach us to adhere to God's plan
and be dedicated to your Son, Jesus.
Help us to deny ourselves in order to gain
the souls of our brothers and sisters.
Let us follow the modest things on earth
and reach the heights of heaven.

In the sixteenth apparition at Lourdes, the Blessed Virgin Mary identified herself to Bernadette as the Immaculate Conception.

PRAYERS FROM THE SAINTS

Mary, Vessel of God's Mysteries

MARY,
you are the vessel and tabernacle containing all Mysteries.
You know what the Patriarchs never knew.
You have experienced what was never revealed to the Angels.
You have heard what the Prophets never heard.
In a word, all that was hidden from the preceding generations
was made known to you.
Even more, most of these wonders depended on you.

St. Gregory the Wonderworker

Mary, Mother of Grace

IT BECOMES you to be mindful of us,
as you stand near Him Who granted you all graces,
for you are the Mother of God
and our Queen.
Help us for the sake of the King,
the Lord God and Master Who was born of you.
For this reason you are called full of grace.

Remember us,
most holy Virgin,
and bestow on us gifts from the riches of your graces,
Virgin full of grace.

St. Athanasius

Call upon Mary

IN DANGERS, in doubts, in difficulties,
think of Mary, call upon Mary.

Let not her name depart from your lips,
never suffer it to leave your heart.

And that you may more surely obtain
the assistance of her prayer,
neglect not to walk in her footsteps.

With her for guide,
you shall never go astray;
while invoking her,
you shall never lose heart;
so long as she is in your mind,
you are safe from deception;
while she holds your hand,
you cannot fall;
under her protection,
you have nothing to fear;
if she walks before you,
you shall not grow weary;
if she shows you favor,
you shall reach the goal.

St. Bernard

Mary, Mother of Mercy

BLESSED Virgin Mary,
who can worthily repay you with praise and thanks
for having rescued a fallen world
by your generous consent!

Receive our gratitude,
and by your prayers obtain the pardon of our sins.
Take our prayers into the sanctuary of heaven
and enable them to make our peace with God.
Holy Mary,
help the miserable,
strengthen the discouraged,
comfort the sorrowful,
pray for your people,
plead for the clergy,
intercede for all women consecrated to God.
May all who venerate you
feel now your help and protection.

Be ready to help us when we pray,
and bring back to us the answers to our prayers.
Make it your continual concern
to pray for the people of God,
for you were blessed by God
and were made worthy
to bear the Redeemer of the world,
Who lives and reigns forever. *St. Augustine of Hippo*

In Honor of Mary, Mother of God

HAIL, Mary, Mother of God,
venerable treasure of the whole universe,
lamp that is never extinguished,
crown of virginity,
support of the true faith,
indestructible temple,

dwelling of Him Whom no place can contain,
O Mother and Virgin!
Through you
all the holy Gospels call blessed
the One Who comes in the name of the Lord.

Hail, Mother of God;
you enclosed under your Heart the infinite God
Whom no space can contain.
Through you
the Most Holy Trinity is adored and glorified,
and the priceless Cross is venerated
throughout the universe.

Through you
the heavens rejoice,
and the Angels and Archangels are filled with gladness.
Through you
the demons are banished,
and the tempter fell from heaven.
Through you
the fallen human race is admitted to heaven.

Hail, Mother of God;
through you
kings rule,
and the Only Begotten Son of God
has become a star of light
to those who were sitting in darkness
and in the shadow of death. *St. Cyril of Alexandria*

Mary, Model of Our Spiritual Life

HOLY Virgin, I beg you:
enable me to receive Jesus from the Spirit,
according to the same process
by which you bore Jesus.

May my soul possess Jesus
thanks to the Spirit
through Whom you conceived Jesus.

May the grace to know Jesus
be granted to me through the Spirit
Who enabled you to know how to possess Jesus
and bring Him forth.

May my littleness show forth
the greatness of Jesus
in virtue of the Spirit
in Whom you recognized yourself
as the handmaid of the Lord,
desiring that it be done to you
according to the word of the Angel.

May I love Jesus
in the Spirit
in Whom you adored Him as your Lord
and looked after Him as your Son.

St. Ildefonsus of Toledo

Mary's Riches for Us

WE ARE poor in Divine gifts,
O Mary,
but through you

we see the riches of kindness offered to us.
Therefore, we say with confidence:
the earth is full of the mercies of the Lord.

Rejected by God
because of the multitude of our sins,
through you we seek Him out again,
rediscover Him,
and are saved.

Therefore, O Mother of God,
grant us your powerful help
so that we may attain salvation.
And obtain for us the aid of your Son,
the sole Mediator necessary with God.

For your magnificence is infinite,
your goodness in helping the needy is inexhaustible,
and the number of your benefits is limitless.

No one achieves salvation except through you,
O most Immaculate One!
No one receives salvation except through you,
O most Chaste One!
And no one obtains mercy except through you,
O most Honored One!

Who would then fail to call you blessed?

I will call you—
who were enriched by your Son and God—
glorious and blessed,
and I will praise you with all generations.

St. Germanus of Constantinople

Mary, Hope of Christians

HAIL Mary,
hope of Christians,
hear the prayer of a sinner who loves you tenderly,
honors you in a special manner,
and places in you the hope of his/her salvation.
I owe you my life,
for you obtain for me the grace of your Son
and you are the sure pledge of my eternal happiness.

I entreat you,
deliver me from the burden of my sins,
take away the darkness of my mind,
destroy the earthly affections of my heart,
defeat the temptations of my enemies,
and rule all the actions of my life.
With you as my guide
may I arrive at the eternal happiness of heaven.

St. John Damascene

The Mother of God Is Our Mother

O BLESSED Lady,
you are the Mother of Justification
and those who are justified;
the Mother of Reconciliation
and those who are reconciled;
the Mother of Salvation
and those who are saved.

What a blessed trust, and what a secure refuge!
The Mother of God is our Mother.

The Mother of the One in Whom alone we hope
and Whom alone we fear
is our Mother! . . .

The One Who partook of our nature
and by restoring us to life
made us children of His Mother
invites us by this to proclaim
that we are His brothers and sisters.

Therefore, our Judge is also our Brother.
The Savior of the world is our Brother.
Our God has become—through Mary—our Brother!

St. Anselm of Canterbury

Our Lady of the Trinity

HOLY Virgin Mary,
there is none like you among women
born in the world.
Daughter and handmaid of the heavenly Father,
the Almighty King,
Mother of our Most High Lord Jesus Christ,
and Spouse of the Holy Spirit,
pray for us to your most holy Son,
our Lord and Master.

Hail, holy Lady,
most noble Queen,
Mother of God, and Mary ever Virgin.
You were chosen by the heavenly Father,
Who has been pleased to honor you
with the presence of His most holy Son
and the Divine Paraclete.

You were blessed with the fullness
of grace and goodness.
Hail, Temple of God,
His dwelling place, His masterpiece, His handmaid.
Hail, Mother of God.
I venerate you for the holy virtues that—
through the grace and light of the Holy Spirit—
you bring into the hearts of your clients
to change them from unfaithful Christians
to faithful children of God. *St. Francis of Assisi*

Prayer in Praise of the Mother of God

MARY, our Mother,
the whole world reveres you
as the holiest shrine of the living God,
for in you the salvation of the world dawned.
The Son of God was pleased
to take human form from you.
You have broken down the wall of hatred,
the barrier between heaven and earth
that was set up by humanity's first disobedience.
In you heaven met earth
when Divinity and Humanity were joined in one person,
the God-Man.

Mother of God, we sing your praises,
but we must praise you even more.
Our speech is too feeble to honor you
as we ought,
for no tongue is eloquent enough
to express your excellence.

Mary, most powerful, most holy,
and worthy of all love!
Your name brings new life,
and the thought of you inspires love
in the hearts of those devoted to you. *St. Bernard*

Mary, Our Queen

MARY, Our Queen,
Holy Mother of God,
we beg you to hear our prayer.
Make our hearts be filled with Divine grace
and resplendent with heavenly wisdom.
Render them strong with your might
and rich in virtue.
Pour down upon us the gift of mercy
so that we may obtain the pardon of our sins.
Help us to live in such a way
as to merit the glory and bliss of heaven.

May this be granted us by your Son, Jesus,
Who has exalted you above the Angels,
has crowned you as Queen,
and has seated you with Him forever on His refulgent throne. *St. Anthony of Padua*

Prayer of Dedication to Mary

VIRGIN, full of goodness,
Mother of Mercy,
I entrust to you my body and my soul,
my thoughts and my actions,
my life and my death.
My Queen,

come to my aid
and deliver me from the snares of the devil.
Obtain for me the grace of loving
my Lord Jesus Christ, your Son,
with a true and perfect love,
and after Him,
O Mary,
of loving you with all my heart
and above all things. *St. Thomas Aquinas*

Prayer for a Happy Death

HOLY Virgin,
I beg of you,
when my soul shall depart from my body,
be pleased to meet and receive it.

Mary,
do not refuse me then the grace
of being sustained by your sweet presence.
Be for me the ladder and the way to heaven,
and finally assure me of pardon and eternal rest.

St. Bonaventure

Mother of Grace

"DO NOT be afraid, Mary,
for you have found favor with God" (Lk 1:30).
Fear not, Mary,
for you have found grace,
not taken it as Lucifer tried to do.
You have found grace,
not lost it as Adam did.

You have found favor with God
because you desired and sought it.
You have found uncreated Grace,
that is, God Himself became your Son,
and with that Grace
you have found and obtained every uncreated good.

St. Albert the Great

Petition to Mary

MOST chaste Virgin Mary,
by that spotless purity
with which you prepared for the Son of God
a dwelling of delight in your virginal womb,
I beg of you to intercede for me
that I may be cleansed from every stain.
Most humble Virgin Mary,
by that most profound humility
by which you deserved to be raised high above all the choirs
of Angels and Saints,
I beg of you to intercede for me
that all my sins may be expiated.

Most amiable Virgin Mary,
by that indescribable love
that united you so closely and inseparably to God,
I beg of you to intercede for me
that I may obtain an abundance of all merits.

St. Gertrude of Helfta

In Praise of Mary

O MARY, Mary, temple of the Trinity.
O Mary, bearer of fire.
O Mary, dispenser of mercy.
O Mary, restorer of human generation,
because the world was repurchased
by means of the sustenance
that your flesh found in the Word.
Christ repurchased the world with His Passion,
and you with your suffering of mind and body.

O Mary, peaceful ocean.
O Mary, giver of peace.
O Mary, fruitful land.
You, O Mary, are that new plant
from which we have the fragrant flower
of the Word, Only Begotten Son of God,
because this Word was sown in you,
O fruitful land.
You are the land and the plant.

O Mary, vehicle of fire,
you bore the fire hidden and veiled
beneath the ash of your humanity.

O Mary, vase of humility,
in which there burns the light of true knowledge
with which you lifted yourself above yourself
and yet were pleasing to the eternal Father;
hence He took and brought you to Himself,
loving you with a singular love.

With this light and fire of your charity
and with the oil of your humility,
you drew and inclined His Divinity to come into you—
although He was first drawn to come to us
by the most ardent fire of His inestimable charity.

Today, O Mary, you have become a book
in which our rule is written.
In you, today, is written the wisdom
of the eternal Father.
In you, today, is manifested
the strength and freedom of human beings.

I say that
the dignity of human beings is manifested
because when I look at you, O Mary,
I see that the hand of the Holy Spirit
has written the Trinity in you,
forming in you the incarnate Word,
the Only Begotten Son of God.

He has written for us the wisdom of the Father,
that is, the Word.
He has written for us His power,
because He was powerful
in effecting this great mystery.
And He has written for us
the clemency of the Holy Spirit,
because only through grace and the Divine clemency
was so great a mystery ordained and accomplished.

But today I ardently make my request,
because it is the day of graces,
and I know that nothing is refused
to you, O Mary.
Today, O Mary, your land has generated
the Savior for us.

O Mary,
blessed are you among women throughout the ages!

St. Catherine of Siena

Prayer of Self-Commendation to Mary

O HOLY Mary,
my Lady,
into your blessed trust and safekeeping
and into the depths of your mercy
I commend my soul and body this day,
every day of my life,
and at the hour of my death.

To you I entrust
all my hopes and consolations,
all my trials and miseries,
my life and the end of my life.
By your most holy intercession
and by your merits,
may all my actions be directed and disposed
according to your will
and the Will of your Divine Son.

St. Aloysius Gonzaga

Prayer of Offering to Mary

MOST Holy Mary,
Virgin Mother of God,
I am unworthy to be your servant.
Yet moved by your Motherly care for me
and longing to serve you,
I choose you this day
to be my Queen, my advocate, and my Mother.
I firmly resolve ever to be devoted to you
and to do what I can
to encourage others to be devoted to you.

My loving Mother,
through the Precious Blood of your Son shed for me,
I beg you to receive me as your servant forever.
Aid me in my actions
and beg for me the grace
never by thought, word, or deed,
to be displeasing in your sight
and that of your most holy Son.
Remember me, dearest Mother,
and do not abandon me at the hour of death.

St. Francis de Sales

Prayer for the Spirit of Mary

MY POWERFUL Queen,
you are all mine through your mercy,
and I am all yours.
Take away from me all that may displease God
and cultivate in me all that is pleasing to Him.

May the light of your faith
dispel the darkness of my mind,
your deep humility
take the place of my pride,
your continual sight of God
fill my memory with His presence.
May the fire of the charity of your Heart
inflame the lukewarmness of my own heart.
May your virtues take the place of my sins.
May your merits be my enrichment
and make up for all
that is wanting in me before God.

My beloved Mother,
grant that I may have no other spirit but your spirit,
to know Jesus Christ and His Divine Will
and to praise and glorify the Lord,
that I may love God with burning love like
yours.

St. Louis de Montfort

Mary, Our Hope for Salvation

MARY, my Hope,
you are my peace!
Whenever I call upon you or think of you,
I experience such great joy
that my heart is completely ravished.
Whenever some worry troubles me,
it vanishes as soon as I utter your name.
On the sea of the world,
you are the bright star that guides my little boat.
And it is under your protection
that I want to live and die . . .

You are my Mother,
for you are the Mother of my God.
What could I fear, O Mary,
if you love me? . . .

You are a Queen that has captured the Heart of God.
If you wish to save us,
say only that we are your children,
and God will have mercy on us!

St. Alphonsus Liguori

Mary, Help of Christians

MARY, powerful Virgin,
you are the mighty and glorious protector of the Church.
You are the marvelous help of Christians.
You are awe-inspiring as an army in battle array.
You eliminated heresy in the world.
Amid our anguish, struggle, and distress,
defend us from the power of the enemy,
and at the hour of our death
receive our soul in heaven.

St. John Bosco

Mary, Our Guide to Heaven

VIRGIN full of grace,
I know that at Nazareth you lived modestly,
without requesting anything more.
Neither ecstasies, nor miracles, nor other extraordinary deeds
enhanced your life,
O Queen of the Elect.

The number of the lowly, "the little ones," is very great on earth.
They can raise their eyes to you
without any fear.
You are the incomparable Mother
who walks with them along the common way
to guide them to heaven.

Beloved Mother,
in this harsh exile,
I want to live always with you
and follow you every day.
I am enraptured by the contemplation of you
and I discover the depths of the love of your Heart.
All my fears vanish under your Motherly gaze,
which teaches me to weep and to rejoice!

St. Thérèse of the Child Jesus

Consecration to Our Lady

IMMACULATE Virgin,
grant that I may praise you
with my total commitment and my personal sacrifice.
Grant that I may live, work, suffer, be consumed, and die for you.

Grant that I may contribute
to an ever greater exaltation of you.
May I render more glory to you
than anyone has ever rendered to you in the past.
Grant that others may surpass me
in zeal for your exaltation

and that I may in turn surpass them.
Thus, in a noble emulation,
your glory may always increase,
in accord with the desire of the One Who exalted you
above all creatures.

In you God is glorified
more than in all His Saints.
Through you God has created the world,
and through you He has called me into existence.

Make me worthy to praise you,
O Immaculate Virgin. *St. Maximilian Kolbe*

TRADITIONAL PRAYERS

Prayer of Veneration

HOLIEST Virgin,
with all my heart I venerate you
above all the Angels and Saints in Paradise
as the Daughter of the Eternal Father,
and I consecrate to you
my soul with all its powers.
Hail Mary, ...

Holiest Virgin,
with all my heart I venerate you
above all the Angels and Saints in Paradise
as the Mother of the Only Begotten Son,
and I consecrate to you
my body with all its senses.
Hail Mary, ...

Holiest Virgin,
with all my heart I venerate you
above all the Angels and Saints in Paradise
as the beloved Spouse of the Holy Spirit,
and I consecrate to you
my heart and all its affections,
praying you to obtain for me from the Most Holy Trinity
all the graces I need for my salvation.
Hail Mary, ...

Prayer of Consecration to Mary

O MY Queen and Mother,
I give myself entirely to you.

To show my devotion to you,
I consecrate to you this day
my eyes, ears, mouth, heart,
and whole being without reserve.

Therefore, good Mother,
since I am your own,
keep me and guard me
as your property and possession.

Prayer for the Grace to Love Jesus

MARY, my dear Mother,
how much I love you—
and yet in reality how little!
You teach me what I should know,
for you instruct me in
what Jesus is for me
and what I should be for Him.

O my beloved Mother,
how close to God you are,
and how completely filled with Him!
To the extent that we know God,
we are reminded of you.
Mother of God,
obtain for me the grace of loving my Jesus
and the grace of loving you.

Prayer to See Jesus through Mary

MOST holy and Immaculate Virgin,
my Mother!
You are the Mother of my Lord,
the Queen of the Universe,

the advocate, hope, and refuge of sinners.
I, the most miserable of sinners,
have recourse to you today.
I venerate you, great Queen,
and I thank you for the many graces
you have bestowed on me until now.
I thank you especially for having saved me from hell,
which I have so often deserved by my many sins.

Most lovable Lady,
I love you,
and by the love I have for you
I promise to serve you always
and to do all I can to make you loved by others.
I place in you all my hope of salvation.
Mother of Mercy,
receive me as your servant
and cover me with the mantle of your protection.
Since you are so powerful with God,
deliver me from all temptations
or rather obtain for me the grace
to overcome them until death.

I ask of you a true love for Jesus Christ.
Through you I hope to die a good death.
My dear Mother,
by the love you have for Almighty God
I beg you to help me always
and especially at the last moment of my life.
Do not leave me until you see me safe in heaven,
where I hope to thank and praise you forever.

Prayer to Mary, Mother of the Church

O BLESSED Virgin Mary,
the basic reason why you are Mother of the Church
is that you are the Mother of God
and the associate of Christ in His saving work.

Another reason is that you shine as the model of virtues
for the whole community of the Elect.
You exemplified in your own life
the Beatitudes preached by Your Divine Son.
Hence, you are the perfect model
for the imitation of Christ
on the part of all human beings.

Obtain for us the graces we need
to follow your example.
Teach us to practice the Beatitudes proper to our state
and to rejoice in being known as your children
who are members of the Church of God.

Let us work for the unity of the Church,
which your Son desired on earth
and which you now pray for in heaven.
Lead the whole human race
to acknowledge Christ Jesus, the one true Savior.
Drive from it all the calamities provoked by sin,
and bring it peace,
which consists in truth, justice, liberty, and love.

Prayer to Emulate Mary's Faith

MARY, our Mother,
you consented in faith
to become the Mother of Jesus.
At the Angel's announcement
you received the Word of God in your Heart
as well as in your body,
and you brought Life to the world.
You conceived in your Heart, with your whole being,
before you conceived in your womb.

Obtain for us
a faith similar to your own,
which will enable us to hear the Word of God
and carry it out.
Let us imitate your Motherhood by our faith,
bringing Christ to birth in others
who have desperate need of Him.

Prayer to Mary Assumed into Heaven

O BLESSED Virgin Mary,
united to the victorious Christ in heaven,
you are the image and first-flowering of the Church
as she is to be perfected in the world to come.
You shine forth as a sign of sure hope and solace
for the pilgrim People of God.
In your Assumption,
you manifest the fullness of redemption
and appear as the spotless image of the Church
responding in joy to the invitation of the Bridegroom,
your Son,

Who is the firstfruits of those who have fallen asleep.

Grant that we may follow your example on earth
thereby imitating your Son as well
and being enabled to share your glory
with Him for all eternity.

Prayer to Mary, Queen of the Home

O BLESSED Virgin Mary,
you are the Mother and Queen of every Christian family.
When you conceived and gave birth to Jesus,
human motherhood reached its greatest achievement.
From the time of the Annunciation
you were the living chalice
of the Son of God made Man.
You are the Queen of the Home.
As a woman of faith,
you inspire all mothers to transmit faith
to their children.

Watch over our families.
Let the children learn free and loving obedience
inspired by your obedience to God.
Let parents learn dedication and selflessness
based on your unselfish attitude.
Let all families honor you
and remain devoted to you
so that they may be held together
by your example and your intercession.

PRAYERS FOR VARIOUS NEEDS, PERSONS, AND SITUATIONS

Abandonment to Mary

VIRGIN, full of goodness,
I entrust my life to you.
If you will not help me, where can I turn?
But all the Saints have said
that you help all your children who go to you,
even the worst sinner.
I pray for myself and all sinners.
I pray for the souls in purgatory.
May your beautiful Motherly care always be with me.
May I be humble as you were humble.
Pride blocks the heart,
and Jesus cannot come in.
May you, O Mother, ever be my model
in humility and resignation to the Will of God.

For Preservation from Sin

O MOTHER of God,
Mary most holy,
how many times I have sinned.
But you, in your kind mercy, have rescued me.
Help me to overcome the hardness of my heart;
gently draw me to place all my trust in you.
Loving Mother,
preserve me from sin by your graces.

O my Queen, I am grateful
for all your many mercies and blessings.
I love you, next to God, above all things.
Permit not that I ever turn my back on you.

Through your intercession,
keep me close to your Divine Son on earth,
that I may rejoice with you forever in heaven.

To Know God's Will

DEAREST Mother,
help me to remember
that I am made in the image and likeness of God.
Grant that all the thoughts of my mind,
all the words of my tongue,
all the affections of my heart,
and all the actions of my being
may always be conformed to the Divine Will.

Between me and God's most distant desire,
let there be no veil that you have not removed,
no barrier that you have not torn down,
no infection that you have not cured,
no door that you have left unopened,
so that you may place my heart
within the radiance of God's knowledge
and make me taste the fragrance of His love.

For Spiritual Strength

HOLY Virgin Mary,
Mother of Jesus and my Mother,
keep me free from sin
and protect me in all dangers of soul and body.
Help me today in my work.
Make me faithful to you
so that I may give glory to God
and save my soul.

To Be Truly Human

DEAR Mother Mary,
your Divine Son embraced our humanity
and so taught us how to be truly human.
Help me to follow His example
and bring out in myself all that is truly human.
Teach me to appreciate the immense good
that lies in being human,
climaxed by the gift of genuine self-giving.

Enable me to make use of all the gifts God has given me
in the way He desires they be used,
especially for the good of others.
Make me realize that only when I am genuinely human
can I be a true follower of your Divine Son.

To Know My Vocation

DEAR Mother Mary,
God selected you to be the Mother of His Son
and to have a definite vocation,
and you freely consented to it
for your good
and the good of the human race.
Make me realize that each of us also has a vocation,
some state in life that God intends for us
for our own good
and the good of the whole human race.

Help me to know my vocation
and to follow it with joy and dedication.
Never let me lose hope,
for God has given me the talents
to succeed in any state to which He calls me.

To Attain Eternal Life

MOTHER of Christ,
I appeal to your mercy
and beg you to pray to your Divine Son for me.
Let me share in the benefits of His sacrifice
that I may be truly sorry for my sins
and save my soul.
I want to belong to His Kingdom.

Help me to live up to the teaching of His Church,
which He founded for the salvation of all.
Through you, we received the Author of Life;
through you, may we reach eternal life.

For a Happy Death

JESUS, Mary, and Joseph,
I give you my heart and my soul.

Jesus, Mary, and Joseph,
assist me in my last agony.

Jesus, Mary, and Joseph,
may I breathe forth my soul in peace with you
in my last agony.

Dedication of a Family to Mary

MOST Blessed Virgin Mary,
I kneel here before you with my family
and choose you
for my Lady, Mother, and advocate with God.
I dedicate myself and all who belong to me
to your service forever.
Take us under your protection.
Help us in life and at the hour of our death.

Bless me and all my family.
Never let any of us offend your Son.
In every temptation defend us.
Protect us in every danger.
Provide for us in the necessities of life.
Comfort us in every sorrow, in every sickness,
and especially in the final sorrow of death.
Grant that we may all enter into heaven
to thank you and, in your company,
to praise and love Jesus, our Redeemer,
for all eternity.

For My Children

MARY, Mother of God,
and Mother of all Christians,
you presented your Divine Son in the Temple.
Now I present to you the children
whom God has graciously given me.
By the grace of their Baptism,
which incorporated them into Christ,
you became their Mother.

I entrust them to you,
to your guidance and vigilance.

Make them healthy in both soul and body.
Help them to become useful citizens
of their own country,
but let them not forget
the Kingdom of God.
If they go astray,
lead them back to your Son
so that they may obtain forgiveness and peace.
Enable us all to reach eternal happiness
with you and your Divine Son in heaven.

For My Parents

MARY, my Mother,
you brought Jesus into this world
and looked after Him
as my parents brought me into this world
and look after my spiritual and material health.
Obtain for them God's choicest blessings
and enrich their souls with grace.
Keep them close to you all their lives
and lead them to Jesus.

May I and their other children be ever
their joy in this life
and their crown of glory in the next.
Bring them to a ripe old age
in health of mind and body
and grant them a holy death
in union with you and your Divine Son.

For My Relatives

MARY, my Mother,
pray for all my relatives.
Grant them health of mind and body.
Make them love God with all their hearts
and practice only those things
that are pleasing to Him.
Keep them safe from all harm
and bring them to your Son's eternal home
after their earthly pilgrimage.

For My Friends

DEAR Mother Mary,
on earth your Son had many close friends.
In this way He showed
that friendship is one of life's greatest blessings.
Help me to appreciate the friends God has given me
to love me in spite of my failures and weaknesses
and to enrich my life.

Bind us close together in you
and enable us to help one another
on our earthly journey
so that we may be in heaven forever
with you and your Divine Son.

For My Birthday

MARY, my Mother,
today is the anniversary of my birth,
the day on which the heavenly Father

allowed me to enter this wonderful world.
Help me to realize that I was put here for a reason:
to know, love, and serve God on earth
and be happy forever with Him in heaven.
Teach me the fleetingness of time
and the enduring length of eternity.
Keep me close to you until my death,
starting from today,
which is the first day of the rest of my life.

For a Good Spouse

MARY Immaculate,
sweet Mother of the young,
I entrust to your special care the decision
that I am to make as to my future husband (wife).
You are my Guiding Star!
Direct me to the person
with whom I can best cooperate
in doing God's holy Will
and with whom I can
live in peace, love, and harmony in this life
and attain to eternal joys in the next.

For Mary's Protection Every Day

HOLY Mother Mary,
I place myself under your loving protection
and ask the help of your intercession.

Immaculate Mary, Morning Star, Star of the Sea,
light the way for me.
May I be cheerful and pleasant to others this day
and especially to those in my own home.

For Help in Trials

HAVE pity on me,
Mother of my Savior,
and grant me consolation in my trials.
Plead my cause before the Lord
and keep me from further worry and pain.
Ask God to pardon me for all my sins;
may your merits and prayers atone for them.
In you are salvation and life,
unending joy and a glorious eternity.

In Time of Worry

DEAR Blessed Mother,
many times I worry and am anxious.
Please take these worries from me,
so that, at peace, I may help others
and think less about myself.
You are the advocate of the most miserable and abandoned;
you are the special friend of sinners.

Help me.
Come to my assistance.
I commend myself to you
and place in your hands all who are in need.

In Time of Sorrow

MOTHER of God,
look down upon a poor sinner
who has recourse to you.
Dear Mother,
I put my trust in you.
You stood beneath the Cross
and saw your Son die for us sinners
because He wished so much to save us.
O good Mother,
O Mother of Mercy,
have pity on us,
your little children.

In Sickness

HOLY Mary, Mother of God,
and my Mother,
I come before you
in the knowledge that you will help me.
My faith tells me so
and my heart makes me sure of this.
In my sickness,
and in the midst of my suffering,
I often call out to you: "Mother!"
Just saying this word
makes me feel better.

When I feel misunderstood and all alone,
I know that you are with me
and that you love me.
Help me, Mary,
and when I am well, let me love God more.

For an Expectant Mother

MARY,
most pure Virgin and Mother of God,
I remind you of the blessed moment
when for the first time
you saw your newborn Child
and enfolded Him in your arms.
Through this joy of your Motherly Heart,
obtain for me the grace
that I and my child may be protected
from all danger.

Mary,
Mother of my Savior,
I remind you of the unspeakable joy you felt
when, after three days of painful seeking,
you again found your Divine Son.
Through this joy,
obtain for me the grace
to bring into the world
a healthy and well-formed child.

Most glorious Virgin Mary,
I remind you of the heavenly joy
that flooded your Motherly Heart
when your Son appeared to you after His Resurrection.
Through this great joy,
obtain for my child
the blessings of holy Baptism,
so that my child may be admitted to the Church,
the Mystical Body of your Divine Son.

For a Woman in Childbirth

HAIL, O Queen of Heaven,
Mother of Mercy,
Consolation of Life,
and Joy of those who love you!
We cry out to you
on behalf of this poor sufferer.

In your Motherly goodness,
take pity on her.
Do not abandon her in her pains,
since she places a childlike confidence in you.
Through your own blessed delivery
and your Divine Son,
stand by her and gladden her with a happy delivery,
that she may gratefully praise your kindness.

In all our troubles and necessities,
we fly to you for help,
O Blessed Virgin Mary.

For the Sick and the Dying

O MOTHER of help,
please assist the sick and the dying.
Give your special love to those who die this day.
Help all the poor souls in purgatory.
Assist all who are in need,
especially those who are hungry in soul and body.
What comfort you bring us!
We are most grateful,
dear Mother.

For the Souls in Purgatory

JESUS, Mary, and Joseph,
give eternal rest to the poor souls.
Jesus, Mary, and Joseph,
let perpetual light shine upon them.
May they rest in peace.

For World Peace

DEAREST Mother,
with all my heart I honor you.
Bless me and guard me,
guide me and keep me.
You are my consolation and my comfort.
Blessed are you.
Break down the walls
of hatred and prejudice in the world
and bring peace for all human beings.

Mother of God,
I sing your praise.
Inspire me to love your Son more.

When Jesus was born, ". . . the Word became flesh and dwelt among us. And we saw his glory . . . ." *John 1:14*

PRAYERS FOR THE LITURGICAL SEASONS

Advent

For Christ's Triple Coming

IMMACULATE Virgin Mary,
your Son once came to rid the world of sin;
may He come to cleanse me of every sin.
Dearest Mother,
Jesus once came to save what was lost;
may He now come again with His saving power
so that those He redeemed will not be punished.
Dearest Mother,
I have come to know your Son in faith;
may I have unending joy when He comes again in glory.

For Christ's Coming in Grace

IMMACULATE Virgin Mary,
during this Advent, may Jesus come to us in grace.
May He come to prepare our hearts, minds, and bodies
to welcome Him on Christmas day.
May He come to comfort us in sadness,
to cheer us in loneliness,
to refresh us in weariness,
to buttress us in temptations,
to lead us in doubt,
and to exult with us in joy.

Christmas Time

For Christ's Rebirth in the Church

VIRGIN Mother of Christ,
we do not ask that Jesus renew for us
His birth according to the flesh.
We ask that He incarnate us
in His invisible Divinity.
May He accomplish now in His Church
what He accomplished corporally in you.
May the Church's sure faith conceive Jesus,
her unstained intelligence give birth to Him,
and her soul united with the power of the Most High,
preserve Him forever.

For Christ to Be Known to All

VIRGIN Mother of Christ,
obtain for us a new Epiphany
when your Son will be manifested to the world:
to those who do not know Him,
to those who do not want Him,
to those who vilify His Name,
to those who oppress His Mystical Body,
to those who deny Him,
and to those who unconsciously long for Him.

Bring the day closer
when all people will know and love Him
with the Father and the Holy Spirit

together with you—
and the Kingdom of God will have arrived.

Ordinary Time

For a Productive Faith

MARY, Woman of Faith,
increase my faith
and let it bear fruit in my life.
Let it bind me fast to other Christians
in the common certitude
that our Master is the God-Man,
your Divine Son, Jesus,
Who gave His life for all.

Let me listen in faith
to the Divine Word that challenges me.
Help me to strive wholeheartedly
under the promptings of my faith
in the building of a world ruled by love.
Enable me to walk in faith
toward the indescribable future
that your Son has promised
to all who possess a productive faith in Him.

Growing with the Church Year

MARY, Mother of the Church,
I know that all human relations take time
if they are to grow and deepen.
This is also true of my relations
with your Son, Jesus; the Father; and the Spirit,

which must grow over the course of my life.
However, this growth is not automatic;
time alone means nothing
unless I add my earnest efforts to it.
Your Divine Son has inspired the Church
to set aside special times
when this growth can develop more intensely—
the special seasons of the Church Year.
Help me to take them seriously
and make a real attempt to use them well,
so that I will grow into the person
that Jesus wants me to be.

Making Use of Frequent Prayer

MARY, Model of Prayer,
let me realize that, like all prayer,
prayer of petition is primarily
a means of encountering God—
the Father, the Son, and the Holy Spirit—
and being sustained by God.
It is also a means of encountering you,
and asking you to intercede with God for us,
for you are the Mother of God's Son
and His most perfect disciple.
It is true that God knows our needs,
but He wants us to express our requests
to Him directly or through you.

Let me pray always
so that I will purify my intentions
and bring them into accord with God's Will.
Let me pray with fixed formulas

as well as in my own words.
I will then come to know and love you more
and in so doing know and love Jesus even more.

Lent

To Be Freed of the Seven Deadly Sins

O QUEEN of Peace,
implant in me the virtues of gentleness and patience.
Let me curb the fury of *anger*
and restrain all resentment and impatience
so as to overcome evil with good,
attain your Son's peace,
and rejoice in His love.

O Model of Humility,
divest me of all *pride* and *arrogance*.
Let me acknowledge my weakness and sinfulness,
so that I may bear mockery and contempt
for the sake of Jesus
and esteem myself as lowly in His sight.

O Teacher of Abstinence,
help me to serve you rather than my appetites.
Keep me from *gluttony*—
the inordinate love of food and drink—
and let me hunger and thirst for God's justice.

O Lover of Purity,
remove all *lust* from my heart,
so that I may serve you with a pure mind
and a chaste body.

O Mother of the Poor,
help me to avoid all *covetousness* for earthly goods
and give me a love for heavenly things.
Inspire me to give to the needy,
just as your Son gave His life
that I might inherit eternal treasures.

O Exemplar of Love,
keep me from all *envy* and ill-will.
Let the grace of God's love dwell in me
that I may rejoice in the happiness of others
and bewail their adversities.

O zealous Mother of Souls,
keep me from all *sloth* of mind or body,
so that I may do all things
for and in you and your Divine Son, Jesus.

To Follow Christ

MARY, Perfect Disciple of Christ,
your Divine Son was gentle and humble of heart,
full of compassion and maker of peace.
He lived in poverty
and suffered persecution for the cause of justice.
He chose the Cross as the path of glory
to show us the way of salvation.
Intercede on my behalf
that I may receive the Word of the Gospel joyfully
and live by His example,
as an heir and citizen of His Kingdom.

Easter Time

For True Faith in Christ

MARY, the First Believer,
on Easter morn,
Jesus rose from the tomb
and appeared to you.
You saw His glorified Body,
touched Him, and worshiped Him.
Help me to believe with all my heart
that Jesus is risen,
that He is reigning
with His glorified Body
and with His Divinity
for all eternity.
Then when my life is ended let me
be united with both of you
in the glory of heaven.

For the Easter Virtues

MARY, the First among the Redeemed,
the Resurrection of Christ your Son
has given me new life and renewed hope.
Help me to live as a new person
in pursuit of the Easter ideal.
Grant me the wisdom to know what I must do,
the will to want to do it
the courage to undertake it,
the perseverance to continue to do it,
and the strength to complete it.

The exemplary life that the Blessed Virgin Mary led on earth merited her crowning as Queen of Heaven.

PRAYERS FOR EVERY DAY

THOSE who are deeply devoted to our Blessed Mother are not of a mind to wait for her feasts or special Marian celebrations before praying to her. They want to pray to Mary every day—and at any given moment. The author of The Imitation of Mary, *a Christian classic, puts this sentiment in words:*

"Let us be careful to profit by the opportunities we have of pleasing Mary. Nothing seems too humble when her service is at stake, for indeed nothing is unimportant when it comes to serving the Mother of God, the Queen of the World. . . . Let us carefully offer her each day the tribute of our praise and the homage of our hearts."

Accordingly, this section offers Marian prayers for each day of the week. These follow the traditional Church pattern of assigning a particular Mystery of Christ to each day of the week. Insofar as possible, the prayers given are those that accord best with the liturgical orientation of each day of the week. This enables Mary's clients to meditate on the pertinent aspect of their faith as they pray to Mary day by day.

Hence, those who use these prayers will be completely in tune with the mind of the Church at any given moment. At the same time, they will get to know Mary in the various stages of her life with Jesus and her present state of glory in heaven. They will obtain a better idea of Mary's role in the Mystery of Redemption, which her Son accomplished for the whole world.

In so doing, Mary's clients will also follow the fervent recommendation of the Church issued through the lips of Pope Pius XI: "By persevering prayer let us make Mary our daily Mediatrix, our true advocate. In this way, we may hope that she herself, assumed into heavenly glory, will be our advocate before Divine Goodness and Mercy at the hour of our passing."

A few "Daily Prayers"—prayers that can be used day after day—conclude this section.

Prayers for Each Day of the Week

Sunday — Our Lady of the Trinity

OUR Lady of the Trinity,
Sunday is the Day of the Lord:
Father, Son, and Holy Spirit.
You are the beloved Daughter of the Father,
devoted Mother of the Son,
and exalted Bride of the Holy Spirit.
Help me to keep Sundays holy
by participating in the Eucharist
and dedicating myself to the things of God.

Grant that all the thoughts of my mind,
all the words of my mouth,
all the affections of my heart,

and all the actions of my life
may always be conformed to the Will of God.

Give me a great faith
to discern God here below.
Then take me at last
to contemplate the ineffable Lord face to face
and to possess Him forever in heavenly glory
in union with you.

Monday — Our Lady of Grace

OUR Lady of Grace,
Monday is the day of the Holy Spirit,
the Sanctifier.
Your soul was made full of grace
by the power of the Holy Spirit,
the third Person of the Trinity,
the uncreated love between the Father and the Son.
Through you I beg the merciful Father
to send the Holy Spirit of grace,
that He may bestow on me His sevenfold gifts.
May He send me the gift of *wisdom*,
which is none other than your Son, Jesus;
the gift of *understanding*,
which will enlighten me;
the gift of *fortitude*,
which will make me able to endure hardship
and overcome fear in the pursuit of good;
the gift of *counsel*,
which will give me the strength to vanquish
the enemies of my sanctification and salvation.

May He impart to me the gift of *knowledge*,
which will enable me to discern
the teaching of your Son, Jesus
and distinguish good from evil;
the gift of *piety*,
which will make me enjoy true peace;
and the gift of *fear of the Lord*,
which will make me shun all iniquity
and avoid all danger of offending
your Divine Son.

Pray for me,
O Lady of the Holy Spirit,
that I may be fruitful in good works
for the glory of God
and the spiritual and material good of all people.

Tuesday — Queen of the Angels and Saints

QUEEN of the Angels and Saints,
Tuesday is the day of the Angels.
Help me to realize that in praising the Angels
I praise God's glory,
for by honoring them,
I honor their Creator,
Who saw fit to send His Angels
to watch over His servants on earth.
Grant that I may be always under their protection
and one day enjoy their company in heaven.

Tuesday is also devoted to the Saints.
Enable me to see that God is glorified in them,
for their glory is the crowning of His gifts.

Mother of our Savior, pray for us.

Mary most pure, pray for us.

By their lives on earth,
He provides me with an example.
By my communion with them,
He gives me their friendship.
By their prayers,
He grants me strength and protection.
By this great company of witnesses,
He spurs me on to victory over evil
and the prize of eternal life.

Dear Mother Mary,
make me share the faith of the Saints on earth,
so that I may also experience their peace in heaven
together with you and your Divine Son.

Wednesday — Spouse of St. Joseph

SPOUSE of St. Joseph,
Wednesday is devoted to your husband,
the saintly carpenter who cared for you and Jesus
as part of the Holy Family.

In honor of this just man
who protected you and Jesus
from Herod, who wanted to kill the Child,
save me from my many sins.
In honor of this foster father of Christ,
the Divine Physician,
sustain the sick and obtain relief for them.
In honor of this gentle man
who died in the arms of you and Jesus,
intercede for the dying.

In honor of this intrepid guardian
of the Holy Family,
protect all Christian families.
In honor of this dedicated and honest workman,
teach me to labor for Jesus.
In honor of this faithful and chaste spouse,
preserve in my heart
a love of fidelity and purity.

Dear Mother Mary,
let me always revere St. Joseph
and imitate his life of total dedication
to you and Jesus.

Thursday — Our Lady of the Blessed Sacrament

OUR Lady of the Blessed Sacrament,
Thursday is devoted to the Blessed Sacrament
in commemoration of the Last Supper,
when Jesus left us the Holy Sacrifice of the Mass,
the memorial of His Passion, Death, and Resurrection.

My Mother Mary,
thank you for having given me the Eucharistic Christ
Who offers Himself to the Father
as the Victim of Calvary at every Mass,
Who gives Himself to me
as food in Holy Communion,
and Who abides with me in the tabernacle
as the best Friend I have in the world.

For this reason I honor you
as Our Lady of the Blessed Sacrament.
Make me a frequent apostle of the Eucharist
and so Eucharist-minded
that my very life may be the Eucharist.

Friday — Our Lady of Sorrows

OUR Lady of Sorrows,
during your life on earth,
you were saddened many times
and specifically during the traditional Seven Sorrows:
the prophecy of Simeon at the Presentation,
the flight into Egypt,
the three days' loss of Jesus,
the meeting with Jesus carrying His Cross,
His Death on Calvary,
His being taken down from the Cross,
and His burial in the tomb.
Your sorrow on Calvary was deeper
than any sorrow felt on earth,
for no mother in all the world
had a heart as tender as your Heart,
which was the Heart of the Mother of God.
You bore your sufferings for us
that we might enjoy the graces of Redemption.

Dear Mother Mary,
console me when I am sad,
and make me happy with your Motherly love.
Comfort me when I am in pain,
and heal the wounds of my spirit.

Fill my heart with your joy,
and make me forget the troubles of this life,
so that I may be happy forever
with you and your Divine Son in heaven.

Saturday — Our Lady, Queen of the World

HAIL, O Mother, Queen of the World.
You are the Mother of Fair Love,
you are the Mother of Jesus,
and the source of all grace,
the fragrance of all virtue,
the mirror of all purity.
You are joy in weeping,
victory in the struggle,
and hope in death.

How sweet is your name in my mouth,
what delightful harmony in my ears,
what intoxication in my heart!
You are the happiness of the suffering,
the crown of Martyrs,
and the beauty of virgins.

Queen of glory and honor,
keep my soul from all danger.
Take my humble prayers
and bring them to God's throne in heaven
that they may be answered.
May I honor you
on earth with all human beings
and in heaven with all the Saints and Angels.

Daily Prayers

Morning Prayer

O MARY, my Queen,
I cast myself in the arms of your mercy.
I place my soul and body
in your blessed care
and under your special protection
today and every day
and above all at the hour of my departure
from this world.
I entrust to you all my hopes and consolations,
all my anguish and misery,
my life and the end of my life.
Through your most holy intercession
and through your merits,
grant that all my works may be directed and carried out
in accord with your will
and the Will of your Divine Son.

St. Louis de Montfort

Evening Prayer

O MARY, my Mother,
by your Motherly prayers,
obtain pardon from Jesus
for the sins I have committed
this day—
in what I have done
and in what I have failed to do.
Help me to do better tomorrow

after a blessed rest
under your watchful eye.
If I should die before I wake,
please beg the Lord my soul to take.

Prayer before Communion

O MARY, my Mother,
you carried in your womb
the God Whom I am going to receive.
Help me by your powerful intercession
to receive Him with humility and love.
Prepare my heart through abundant grace
for the worthy reception
of the Body and Blood of Jesus.

On earth you were so steadfast in His love.
Invest me with your merits
and adorn me with your virtues.
Let me share in your good works,
that the Lord of Heaven may find me
richly endowed with merit
and pleasing in His eyes.

Prayer after Communion

MOST holy Mother,
now that I have received Jesus
in His holy Sacrament of love,
unite my soul to His Soul
and my being to His Being.
You gave the form to your Infant God
when He took our human nature;

make me over
according to the likeness of your Son.

Place my poor weak heart in His Heart,
that it may be filled with His sentiments
and His charity.
Let me think as Jesus thought
and let me always act in word and deed
as He did—
in humility, simplicity, and love.
Obtain the same for all those
to whom I am united by any bonds, human or Divine,
that all of us may become pleasing
in your sight
and the sight of God.

"[Jesus] said to his mother, 'Woman, behold, your son.' Then he said to the disciple, 'Behold, your mother.' " *John 19:26-27*

PRAYERS AND INVOCATIONS

The Immaculate Conception

Prayer for a Holy Life

VIRGIN Immaculate,
Mother of God and my Mother,
from your throne in heaven,
turn your merciful eyes upon me.
With full confidence in your goodness and power,
I beg you to help me in this journey of life,
which is strewn with dangers for my soul.

I entrust myself completely to you,
that I may never be the devil's slave through sin,
but may always live a humble and pure life.
I consecrate my heart to you forever,
since my sole desire is to love your Divine Son, Jesus.
O Mary,
since none of your devoted servants has ever perished,
let me too attain salvation.

The Sorrowful Mother

Prayer to Grow in Grace through Sorrows

MOST holy Virgin and Mother,
your soul was pierced by a sword of sorrow
in the Passion of your Divine Son,

and in His glorious Resurrection
you are filled with never-ending joy at His triumph.
Obtain for us who call upon you
the grace to partake in the trials of the Church
and the sorrows of the Pope,
so that we may be found worthy to grow in grace
and rejoice with them in the consolations
for which we pray,
in the love and peace of the same Christ our Lord.

The Immaculate Heart of Mary

Prayer of Confidence in the Immaculate Heart

MARY Immaculate,
our Mother and Consolation,
with confidence I take refuge in your most loving Heart.
You shall be the dearest object
of my love and veneration.
I shall always have recourse to you
who are the dispenser of the treasures of heaven,
that I may have peace in my sorrows,
light in my doubts,
protection in dangers,
and help in all my needs.

Be, therefore, my refuge, strength, and consolation,
O Mary, the Consoler.
At the hour of my death,
graciously receive the last sighs of my heart

and obtain for me a place in your heavenly home,
where all hearts will praise with one accord
the adorable Heart of Jesus
as well as your most lovable Heart forever.
Our tender Mother,
Comforter of the afflicted,
pray for us who have recourse to you.

Invocations to Mary

O MARY, conceived without sin,
pray for us who have recourse to you.

* * *

REMEMBER, O Virgin Mother of God,
as you stand in the sight of the Lord,
to speak for us, your little children.

* * *

PRAY for us, O Holy Mother of God,
that we may be worthy of the promises of Christ.

On the Miraculous Medal, within a frame formed around the Blessed Virgin Mary, are the words: "O Mary, conceived without sin, pray for us who have recourse to you."

INDEX OF PRAYERS

Devotions

Litanies

Novenas

Popular Prayers

Prayers and Invocations

Prayers for Every Day

Prayers for the Liturgical Seasons

Prayers for Various Needs, Persons, and Situations

Prayers from the Saints

Prayers in Honor of Our Lady's Titles

Traditional Prayers

ISBN 978-1-958237-31-1
90000
9 781958 237311